ONLINE AND SOCIAL MEDIA LAW

For content writers, web editors,
journalists, bloggers, PRs and
anyone who publishes on the internet

Cleland Thom

David Porter

ONLINE AND SOCIAL MEDIA LAW

For permission requests send an email to
cleland@collegeofmediaandpublishing.co.uk
or
d.porter@mmu.ac.uk
titled 'Attention: Permissions'

Cover design and formatting: Clean Copy Publishing

Published by Clean Copy Publishing
cleancopy.co.uk
cleancopypublishing@gmail.com

All content enquiries to
cleland@collegeofmediaandpublishing.co.uk
or
d.porter@mmu.ac.uk

First published 2019

ISBN: 9781687279828

About the authors

Cleland Thom is a consultant in media and internet law.

Visit:

> http://www.clelandthom.co.uk/legal-services/

David Porter is a senior lecturer in journalism at Manchester Metropolitan University. He specialises in teaching media law.

Contact David at:

> d.porter@mmu.ac.uk

> @daveporterdp

Dedications

Cleland: to my sons, Olly, Barney and Jake, who give me so much friendship, help and support, both in my professional and personal life.

David: to my family for their forbearance while I was writing this book. To Cleland for insight, patience and inviting me on board for this project.

Acknowledgments

Our grateful thanks go to Jennie Harborth, of Clean Copy Publishing, who published this book, and to Rachel Finnegan, of Irish Academic Editing, who proofread it.

ABBREVIATIONS

Abbreviations used throughout this book are:

UK	United Kingdom
EU	European Union
US	United States of America
Ipso	Independent Press Standards Organisation
Ofcom	Office of Communications

All other abbreviations are addressed per chapter and are listed in the Appendix.

CONTENTS

ONLINE AND SOCIAL MEDIA LAW

For content writers, web editors, journalists, bloggers, PRs and anyone who publishes on the internet

CHAPTER 1

INTRODUCTION

The internet caught the UK's legal system unawares. Legal precedents and statutes, some dating back centuries, suddenly had to apply to modern technology. Many of them were inadequate, and the courts and the government have spent the last 20 years or so catching up.

A publisher used to be someone who published books, newspapers or magazines. Now, anyone who runs a blog, comments on a forum, or posts on Twitter is a publisher and is subject to many of the same laws as journalists.

The public is now getting used to the fact that internet publishing is not some virtual wild west, where anything goes.

What Happened to Free Speech?

Publishing has more laws and regulations restricting what can be said and published than almost any other sector and, therefore, the concept of 'free speech' is a myth.

In the UK, people can only write freely after first complying with a significant number of laws. Journalists also have to contend with a range of regulatory requirements.

For instance, the media's right to publish people's personal information and photos has been curtailed since the European Convention on Human Rights (ECHR) was introduced into UK law by the Human Rights Act 1998.

This has hit journalism particularly hard. Journalists over the age of 50 will recall a 'golden' era when the media was relatively free to 'publish and be damned'. Now, many would reword this phrase as 'be damned – and then publish'.

The rise of pre-publication injunctions and non-disclosure agreements, where employees are forbidden to speak to the media – as evidenced in the case involving the Telegraph Media Group and Sir Philip Green – places new and worrying restrictions on journalists.

(Courts and Tribunals Judiciary, 2019, *Arcadia Group Ltd, Topshop/Topman Limited and Sir Philip Green v Telegraph Media Group Ltd (Discontinuance)*).

The use of privacy law to restrict the reporting of crime and arrests (as seen in the ZXC v Bloomberg and Sir Cliff Richard OBE v BBC cases), so that all pre-charge investigations are essentially seen as private matters, is another worrying development.

(Inforrm, 2019, *Case Law: ZXC v Bloomberg, Publication of Investigation into Businessman Was a Misuse of Private Information.*)

(Courts and Tribunals Judiciary, 2018, *Sir Cliff Richard OBE v BBC.*)

Journalists must now consider, before publication, whether their words, photos and other content could breach people's privacy rights and, if they do, whether demonstrable public interest exists.

A journalist's cause is not helped by the fact that the definition of public interest, used by the media regulator's Independent Press Standards Organisation (Ipso) and the Office of Communications (Ofcom), and by the Data Protection Act (DPA), is stricter than that used in English common law prior to the introduction of the ECHR.

Lord Denning, as master of the rolls, said in 1969, in the Court of Appeal judgment in the case of London Artists Ltd v Littler, that public interest should not be confined within narrow limits.

He said: "Whenever a matter is such as to affect people at large so that they may be legitimately interested in, or concerned at, what is going on or what may happen to them or others, then it is a matter of public interest, on which everyone is entitled to make honest comment" (UK

Parliament House of Lords, n.d., *Judgments – Reynolds v Times Newspapers Limited and Others*).

This discrepancy was dealt with, to a limited extent, by a revision of the Ipso Editors' Code of Practice, introduced on 1 January 2016.

However, the code only applies to publications that have signed up to be regulated by Ipso.

Many news websites and online news portals and blogs are only regulated by their own complaints procedures – if any.

The latest version of the code can be viewed here: *https://www.ipso.co.uk/editors-code-of-practice/*

(Ipso, 2019, *Editors' Code of Practice*.)

The revision extended the scope of the public interest defence, which now may be available to Ipso-regulated media in the following circumstances:

- Detecting or exposing crime or the threat of crime, or serious impropriety.

- Protecting public health or safety.

- Protecting the public from being misled by an action or statement of an individual or organisation.

- Disclosing a person or an organisation's failure, or likely failure, to comply with any obligation to which they are subject.

- Disclosing a miscarriage of justice.

- Raising or contributing to a matter of public debate, including serious cases of impropriety, unethical conduct, or incompetence concerning the public.

- Disclosing concealment, or likely concealment, of any of the above.

However, the public interest defence also presents a high threshold for journalists. The code states: "Editors invoking the public interest will need to demonstrate that they reasonably believed publication – or journalistic activity taken with a view to publication – would both serve, and be proportionate to, the public interest and explain how they reached that decision at the time" (Ipso, 2019, Editors' Code of Practice).

This means that journalists must be certain what the public interest issue is, when they begin investigating a story and must be able to back up their decision with evidence.

This can pose problems for investigative journalists, who sometimes need to carry out preliminary enquiries to determine whether a story stands up. They may not be certain if there is a public interest issue at this stage.

There is No Right to Free Speech

In addition, the UK does not provide any legal or constitutional guarantee for safeguarding free speech or the free press.

This contrasts with the US, where the First Amendment of the US Constitution sets out that: "Congress shall make no law […] abridging the freedom of speech, or of the press

[…]" (National Constitution Center, n.d., *Amendment I Freedom of Religion, Speech, Press, Assembly, and Petition*).

But UK content writers, journalists and online publishers must contend with dozens of pieces of legislation and several regulatory codes.

This book looks at online and social media laws and regulation against a background where the press is more heavily restricted than it has ever been.

This is borne out by the fact that the UK is listed 33rd in the 2019 World Press Freedom Index (Reporters without Borders, 2019, *World Press Freedom Index*).

This is an improvement on the 2018 position of 40th, but the UK is still behind countries such as Ghana, Namibia and Uruguay and can certainly no longer be touted as a bastion of free speech.

However, those who blame the constraints of European law and the ECHR for the UK's ranking should bear in mind that around half of the EU's member states appear higher than the UK.

We live in a febrile atmosphere with increasing intolerance and political correctness. The testing of the limits of free speech was shown in May 2019, when comedian Jo Brand came in for heavy criticism when she jokingly suggested, on a Radio 4 programme, that people should throw battery acid over politicians in the street.

The comments were investigated by the police after Brexit party leader Nigel Farage claimed her words amounted to inciting hate and constituted a crime.

In 2017, Freedom House, an independent freedom watchdog, published a report titled New Report: Freedom of the Press 2017 – Press Freedom's Dark Horizon (Freedom House, 2017, *New Report: Freedom of the Press 2017 – Press Freedom's Dark Horizon*).

The report found that only 13% of the world's population enjoys a free press, 45% of the population lives in countries designated as 'not free' in terms of the media, and politicians in supposedly democratic countries such as Poland and Hungary use 'friendly private outlets' to shape the news agenda.

The Impact of Brexit

It is impossible to predict if, when or how the UK will leave the EU, and the situation sometimes changes by the day.

Readers will have to bear with us if events have overtaken the content of this chapter.

EU law will continue to apply in the UK until the UK leaves the EU. However, the legal situation after that depends on the outcome of the UK's Brexit final withdrawal agreement, if any, and any accompanying political declaration, or any 'no-deal' agreement.

The government introduced the European Union (EU) (Withdrawal) Act in 2018. This was formerly known as the 'great repeal bill', and seeks to end the authority of EU law by converting all its provisions into British law when and if the UK leaves the EU.

Details of the Act can be found here:
http://www.legislation.gov.uk/ukpga/2019/16/contents/enacted

The 1972 European Communities Act will simultaneously be repealed.

After that, it is almost certain that the UK will allow existing EU laws to remain in place unless there is a need to change them. If there is, then parliament will introduce new legislation over time.

The reality is that Brexit is unlikely to have any significant effect on UK online and social media laws in the medium term. The main affected areas are copyright, trademarks, data protection, defamation and the ECHR.

Let us look at these in turn.

Copyright

The EU has shaped UK copyright law, especially over the past 15 years, both through legislation and EU court decisions.

For instance, in 2015, the European Court of Justice (ECJ) ruled in the case of Pez Hejduk v EnergieAgentur that photographers can sue for copyright breaches in the UK courts if their photos are used in another EU country. In the past, actions had to be brought in the country where the photos were published.

It is unclear whether historic ECJ rulings like this will carry any weight post-Brexit. The UK will certainly not be bound by future rulings if it leaves the EU.

Much UK copyright law has been derived from EU directives that have been implemented through UK legislation.

Although the withdrawal will end the jurisdiction of the ECJ in the UK, these directives will remain the same, unless parliament repeals them or introduces new legislation. However, this is unlikely, given the global nature of copyright in the digital age.

The UK will not have to implement future directives, and that could be significant in the long term.

However, it is important to remember that many UK copyright principles are based on international treaties that go beyond the EU.

The UK will remain a member of the World Intellectual Property Organisation, a global forum for intellectual property services and cooperation among UN members. As a result, fundamental change is unlikely.

The government's latest guidance – IP and Brexit: The Facts – issued in 2019, states: "While the UK remains in the EU, our copyright laws will continue to comply with the EU copyright directives, and we will continue to participate in EU negotiations" (GOV.UK, 2019, *IP and Brexit: The Facts*).

To guard against a no-deal Brexit, the government brought in legislation in 2018 called the Intellectual Property (Copyright and Related Rights) (Amendment) (EU Exit) Regulations 2019, which outlines the possible impact of Brexit for organisations.

It guarantees 1.7m 'comparable UK rights' covering EU trademarks and community designs that will be automatically transferred, if and when the UK leaves the EU.

In addition, the withdrawal agreement signed off by Theresa May, when she was prime minister, addresses intellectual property but does not specifically mention copyright.

The withdrawal agreement provides for a transition period from the date of exit up until 31 December 2020, and the laws of the EU will continue to apply during this time.

The situation regarding the implementation of the EU's Digital Single Market Copyright Directive will also be determined by the outcome of the Brexit process.

The Intellectual Property Office (IPO) has told the legal news website Out-Law: "If the UK does implement this measure, any changes will need to be subject to a full and thorough consultation and robust impact assessment.

"The government will work with interested individuals and businesses to ensure these proposals are implemented in a way which works for the British economy and which strikes an appropriate balance between the interests of the affected parties" (Pinsent Masons, 2019, *UK Approach on EU Copyright Reforms Depends on Brexit*).

Some aspects of the directive would benefit UK media.

It guarantees its revenue streams and gives press publishers what is known as 'a neighbouring right'.

This is similar to the rights enjoyed by musicians, who receive payment when their music is played in TV and radio broadcasts or in public places such as shops, restaurants and nightclubs.

The law has also provided a right for authors of press publications to receive an appropriate share of revenue generated by press publishers in the digital space.

Trademarks

EU trademarks will no longer be applicable in the UK, post-Brexit, and will apply only to countries within the EU.

But it is expected that UK law will be amended to provide equivalent trademark rights in the UK with the same specifications, priority dates and terms as specified in the current EU arrangements.

In March 2019, the government issued guidance on design and trademarks if the EU leaves without a deal. The guidance assures businesses that EU design and mark rights will be "immediately and automatically transferred to the UK" (GOV.UK 2019, *Changes to Design and Trademark Law*).

Cookies

The use of cookies in websites operated within the EU is governed by the *EU Cookies Directive*.

However, it is currently being overhauled and a new ePrivacy Regulation (EPR) is expected in 2020-2021. It was due to come into force in 2018, to sit alongside the GDPR, but deadlines were missed.

In the meantime, the UK has introduced its own update, which requires website operators to make a number of changes. See the _Cookies_ section.

If the UK does not leave the EU, or if the final withdrawal agreement includes compliance with the EPR, then it can expect to make another set of changes in a year or two.

Defamation

User comments on message boards are currently protected by the EU Electronic Commerce Directive (ECD) Regulations 2002.

(GOV.UK, 2002, _EU Electronic Commerce Directive (ECD) Regulations._)

This law means that publishers are not liable if a user defames someone or breaks another law, provided the publisher:

- Does not moderate or edit the content, and

- Operates a 'report and remove' system, where offensive posts are removed quickly on receipt of a complaint.

If the UK decides not to continue with the ECD, then defamatory comments will not be affected, as its own Defamation Acts of 1996 and 2013 provide similar defences.

However, the UK would need to introduce its own Act extending 'report and remove' to breaches of other laws.

This might be a good thing, as there are signs that the EU may water down the ECD's protection. This situation must

be seen alongside a surprise decision by the European
Court of Human Rights (ECtHR) in the case of Delfi AS v
Estonia (ECtHR, 2015, *Delfi AS v Estonia*).

This case, coupled with the possibility of the EU
introducing a 'duty of care' for website operators, may
mean that the UK could decide to introduce a law that
preserves the existing arrangements on non-moderation
and 'report and remove'.

The European Convention on Human Rights (ECHR)

European citizens possess the right to freedom of
expression under the ECHR, but this freedom has
limitations.

On the one hand, Article 10 says: "Everyone has the right
to freedom of expression. This right shall include freedom
to hold opinions and to receive and impart information and
ideas without interference by public authority [...]" (UK
Legislation, n.d., *Human Rights Act*).

However, the ECHR also says: "The exercise of these
freedoms, [...] may be subject to such formalities,
conditions, restrictions or penalties as are prescribed by law
and are necessary in a democratic society, in the interests of
national security, territorial integrity or public safety, [...]
for the protection of the reputation or rights of others, for
preventing the disclosure of information received in
confidence [...]" (UK Legislation, n.d., *Human Rights Act*).

It is too early to predict how Brexit will affect the UK's relationship with the ECHR, and how any changes will affect the media.

THE MEDIA'S REGULATORY BODIES

Press regulation in the UK is in a curious position.

IMPRESS is the 'official' regulator but, in reality, it has little role or influence.

The Leveson inquiry into media standards recommended, in November 2012, that press regulation needed to be beefed up with a Royal Charter to give it the power to investigate and arbitrate on a whole range of laws, and award exemplary damages.

The charter was awarded to IMPRESS.

However, most national newspapers and regional media groups boycotted it and set up Ipso.

To make things even more complicated, some national media – including the Financial Times, The Guardian and the Observer – boycotted Ipso, and set up their own complaints procedures.

IMPRESS, unlike Ipso, is fully compliant with the Leveson inquiry's recommendations. However, it only regulates around 120 free local newspapers, blogs and magazines.

IMPRESS's Standards Code can be seen here: *https://impress.press/standards/*

So in reality, Ipso regulates most UK newspapers and magazines and their websites, including videos.

Ofcom regulates commercial radio and TV. The BBC's editorial content is subject to the Ofcom Broadcasting Code (Ofcom code) in areas such as fairness, privacy, protection of under-18s, and harm and offence.

Independent Press Standards Organisation (Ipso)

Ipso replaced the Press Complaints Commission in 2014, following recommendations made by the Leveson inquiry.

Ipso administers the Editors' Code of Practice and investigates and rules on alleged breaches. It has the power to:

- Monitor printed media and their websites.

- Mediate and adjudicate complaints about breaches of the code.

- Require publication of corrections and adjudications.

- Issue fines for serious and systemic failings.

- Intervene on behalf of the public over privacy and harassment issues.

Publishers must provide complaints procedures and ensure that management and editorial staff members know how to apply them.

If Ipso receives a complaint, it makes an initial assessment to see if the complaint is within its remit and if there may have been a breach of the Editors' Code of Practice.

If it appears that there has, it usually refers the complainant to the publication to deal with under its own complaints procedures. The publication's editor must deal with more serious complaints within a 28-day deadline.

If the complainant and the editor cannot reach an agreement, Ipso will investigate and may adjudicate in the event of a possible breach of the code.

Landmark adjudications by the PCC may also still be relevant unless they have been superseded.

Ipso has published a book called The Editors' Codebook, which explains how it has interpreted the Editors' Code of Practice and sets out best practice guidelines for journalists.

The Editors' Codebook can be downloaded as a pdf here:

https://www.editorscode.org.uk/the_code_book.php

The codebook states that although Ipso is not bound by previous PCC decisions, key PCC rulings are included where they are still relevant.

In February 2016, Ipso asked retired civil servant Sir Joseph Pilling to review its independence, effectiveness and funding.

Sir Joseph published his report, The External Ipso Review, in October 2016. It made nearly 50 recommendations covering most aspects of the regulator's work.

The External Ipso Review report can be downloaded here:

https://www.ipso.co.uk/media/1278/ipso_review_online.pdf

Case Study

In January 2019, Ipso ruled that the Mail Online had breached the privacy of singer Stacey Solomon's family by publishing pictures taken at her sister's wedding.

It ruled that the singer's family had a reasonable expectation of privacy at a private wedding function and that Mail Online's publication of images of the wedding party, including a picture of Stacey Solomon smoking, and adjusting her sister's wedding dress, were intrusive.

Pictures of children at the wedding party, despite being pixelated, were also found to be in breach of clause 6 regarding children.

(Ipso, 2018, 05768-18 *Solomon v Mail Online.*)

(BAILII, 2019, EWHC 1469 (QB).)

Office of Communications (Ofcom)

Ofcom provides detailed guidelines intended for the maintenance of TV and radio broadcasting standards, and also deals with complaints.

As mentioned above, the BBC's content standards now come under the remit of Ofcom which, in its first report on the broadcaster in 2018, stated that the corporation was generally delivering quality programming "through the breadth and quality of its output" (Ofcom, 2018, *Ofcom's annual report on the BBC*).

The Ofcom code can be downloaded here:

http://stakeholders.ofcom.org.uk/broadcasting/broadcast-codes/broadcast-code/

CHAPTER 2

DEFAMATION

Defamation is a constant risk for online publishers.

For example, in February 2019, the Sun was successfully sued by Labour MP and shadow justice secretary Richard Burgon over allegations printed online that he was part of a heavy metal band that "delights in Nazi symbols".

The Sun had claimed that Mr Burgon was friends with and occasionally played for the band Dream Troll, which had reproduced Nazi SS iconography on an album cover.

In fact, the judge in the case, Mr Justice Dingemans, said that the Dream Troll album cover image "was produced as a form of tribute to or imitation of the Black Sabbath album cover" (Courts and Tribunals Judiciary, 2019, *Richard Burgon MP v News Group Newspapers and Thomas Newton Dunn*).

The online version of the story made no reference to the Black Sabbath album cover and remained online despite a complaint from Mr Burgon.

This case demonstrates one of the key areas of defamation law: the meanings of words.

What is Defamation?

Defamation law exists to protect people and businesses from untrue attacks on their moral or professional reputations.

If anyone publishes a statement claiming, for example, that someone is involved in criminal, unprofessional or antisocial behaviour, the publisher can be sued and may have to pay substantial court damages, unless they can prove that the allegations are substantially true.

Case Study

In 2019, Redrow housing boss Steve Morgan sued over an article in the Daily Mail which claimed he had acted in a "greedy, unethical and morally unacceptable way" by buying Redrow houses, intended for affordable homes, and then renting them out himself.

The court found that he had in fact paid over the odds for the homes for which the company could not find suitable buyers.

(Inforrm, 2019, *Morgan v Associated Newspapers: Libel Claim Settled with Apology, Substantial Charity Payment and Statement in Open Court, Four Lessons Learned for Libel Practitioners.*)

(BAILII, 2018, EWHC 1725.)

Defamation cases usually involve statements such as:

- She is a liar.

- He has committed a crime.

- She took a bribe.

- He misused his position for personal gain.

- She is violent or abusive.

- He is a paedophile.

- She had an illicit affair.

- He took illegal drugs.

A person who starts a libel action is called the claimant, and the person defending it is called the defendant. Cases are tried without a jury unless a court orders otherwise.

What is a Defamatory Statement?

The Defamation Act (DA) 2013 maintains that a statement is defamatory if, on the balance of probability, it has caused, or is likely to cause, serious harm to the claimant's reputation (UK Legislation, n.d., *Defamation Act 2013*).

The DA raised the threshold for a libel claim from causing 'harm' to causing 'serious harm'.

There was some uncertainty about what difference this would make, as most pre-DA libel claimants had probably already taken the view that defamatory publications caused them serious harm.

It was expected that the higher threshold would reduce the number of libel cases coming to court.

However, research appears to show that there has been a recent increase in defamation claims.

Figures from the Royal Courts of Justice show that there were 265 claims for defamation in the High Court in 2018 compared with 156 in 2017 and 112 in 2016.

A report on the legal website, Out-Law, states: "The ever-increasing use of the internet as a platform to allow more and more people to, in effect, become publishers is likely to mean that there will be a steady trickle of defamation claims" (Pinsent Masons, 2018, *Defamation claims on the rise in London*).

Commentators attribute the rise in defamation cases to the absence of jury trials, to social media, and to an increasing number of internet users worldwide.

A defamatory statement is one that tends to:

- Cause someone to be shunned or avoided.

- Lower them in the eyes of right-thinking people.

- Expose them to ridicule, hatred and contempt.

- Disparage them in their office, trade or profession.

Case Study

The words 'tend to' are important and were given new meaning by a Supreme Court decision in 2019.

The court gave what should prove to be a definitive ruling on the interpretation of the 'serious harm' definition of section 1(1) of the DA.

The claimant in the case, Bruno Lachaux, was in dispute with his ex-wife over custody of their children.

Various allegations about his behaviour were made in several UK newspapers, which he subsequently sued for libel.

The case went to appeal, with the Evening Standard and the Independent arguing that the test of 'serious harm' to Mr Lachaux's reputation had not been met under section 1.

The Court of Appeal dismissed the newspapers' appeal and pointed to the "inherent tendency" of the words to cause damage to his reputation.

However, five Supreme Court judges dismissed the appeal, ruling that section 1 should be tested not just against a tendency to cause harm to someone's reputation, but against the facts of harm as well.

So the verdict was based on not just likely harm, but evidential harm and its impact on the claimant.

The court reinforced the point that section 1 of the 2013 Act created a higher threshold for defamation and that the extent of damage is now part of the test for a defamatory statement.

The harm caused may have been in the past, or a future one: in the words of the Act, it applies if it "has caused, or is likely to cause" serious harm.

(BAILII, 2019, UKSC 27, *on appeal from* BAILII, 2017, EWCA Civ 1334.)

Case Study

Philosopher AC Grayling was awarded damages of £20,000 in 2019 after prominent Brexiteer Peter North accused him on Twitter of possessing child pornography.

The allegations remained on North's Twitter feed for seven days, where they could be seen by his 7,900 followers.

(Brett Wilson, 2019, *Brexiteer Ordered to Pay Philosopher £20,000 in Libel Damages for Paedophile Tweet.*)

Case Study

In 2018, parish councillor and blogger Patrick Smith was sued for defamation by property developer Stephen Doyle after Smith accused him in his online community newspaper of being involved in fraud and being arrested by police.

Mr Justice Warby said of Smith that he "found him to be a careless journalist who acted with a closed mind and in some respects irrationally".

Smith was ordered to pay damages of £37,500 and was served with an injunction not to repeat the allegations.

(BAILII, 2018, EWHC 2935.)

Case Study

In the case of Theedom v Nourish Training, (BAILII, 2015, EWHC 3769), Judge Moloney gave the following guidelines. He said that serious harm:

- Must be proved, on top of all previous common law requirements for a libel action.
- Relates to reputation, not injury to feelings.
- Can be established with or without evidence.

Claimants can try to establish it without evidence from the level of the defamatory meaning of the words, and the nature and extent of the publication.

It seems certain that claimants will stand a better chance of establishing 'scriousness' if they can provide evidence unless seriousness is obvious from the words and their context.

Who Can Start a Defamation Action?

Any individual can sue any other living individual for defamation. Libelling dead people, a rarely-used criminal offence, was abolished by the Ministry of Justice (MoJ) in July 2009.

Case Study

In 2014, the ECtHR ruled that a libellous attack on a dead person could damage the surviving family's reputation, to the point where it interfered with their private life, in breach of Article 8 of the ECHR.

This was the decision in the case brought against Ukraine by Mr Vladlen Putistin over an article that indirectly criticised his dead father's role in the infamous 'world war two death march', which inspired the famous film Escape to Victory.

(ECtHR, 2013, *Case of Putistin v Ukraine*.)

A business can sue if a statement has caused, or is likely to cause it, serious financial loss. However, it must be able to prove its losses. Therefore, a publisher facing a libel threat from a business may be able to request details about the losses.

Again, this area of the DA will remain unclear until there are more rulings by the courts.

Case Study

Brett Wilson, a firm of solicitors, was defamed on a website called Solicitors from Hell.

The solicitors produced little evidence of serious financial loss other than that of one client withdrawing their custom, and the fact that the offending article appeared within the top five on Google searches for six months.

However, the court accepted this as sufficient proof; it did not require more substantial evidence such as company accounts.

(BAILII, 2015, EWHC 2628.)

Case Study

High-class dating agency Seventy Thirty was sued by wealthy divorcee Tereza Burki after she said its claims to be able to match people with partners were false.

For its part, the firm counter-sued for libel because of unflattering online reviews Burki had written.

While Burki was awarded more than £13,000 in damages for distress, (£12,600 of which was a refund of her original fees), Seventy Thirty was awarded libel damages of £5,000 for a Google review she had posted of the firm's operations.

(BAILII, 2018, EWHC 1570.)

Three Types of Defamation

Defamation law in England and Wales is separated into three areas:

1. **Libel:** an allegation published in written or permanent form. This includes webpages, email messages, faxes, and radio and TV broadcasts. In the online environment, a libellous statement could be published as a:

   - Tweet and retweet or direct message.

   - Facebook chat, wall post or direct message.

   - Blog post or online article.

- Post on a message board or forum.

- Video or audio recording.

2. **Slander:** an allegation made in a transitory, non-permanent form such as speech. Slander cases are rare.

3. **Malicious falsehood:** an allegation that falls short of damaging someone's reputation but is still harmful.

    For instance, it would not be defamatory to say that a famous singer had cancelled a concert because she had pneumonia.

    However, if the statement was false it could affect her earnings.

    She could sue if the publisher knew it was false or had not bothered to check the facts.

Libel is the most common form of defamation, partially because claimants must prove financial loss in cases of slander and malicious falsehood.

What a Libel Claimant Must Prove

A claimant must prove three things to succeed in a libel action:

1. **Defamation:** that the words defamed them. This means that 'a reasonable person' would believe that, on the balance of probabilities, the words caused, or were likely to cause, them serious harm.

2. **Identification**: that the words referred to them. The test for identification is to whom the reasonable person or a friend of the claimant (someone who knows them already), would assume the words referred.

    There is no safety in not naming someone, giving clues to who they are, or using nicknames. In fact, vague identification or non-identification can be more dangerous, as this can allow other people with similar details to bring libel actions.

    It is also possible to libel identifiable groups of people.

    For example, saying that 'architecture lecturers at Banshaw University have been fiddling students' exam grades' means that all the lecturers in that department could sue, even though none of them has been named.

    However, class actions are unlikely to succeed if the group exceeds more than about 12 to 15 people.

Case Study

The internet has created a situation where it is possible to libel someone without naming them, or identifying them at all.

Former Chelsea and England defender Ashley Cole was the first person to claim 'jigsaw identification' in a libel case.

In 2006, the News of the World (NoW) ran a story headlined "Gay as you Go". It alleged that two

Premiership footballers (one capped several times for England) and a music industry figure were caught on camera involved in a "homosexual orgy" (Shoffman, 2006, *Ashley Cole Files Lawsuit over Gay Orgy Story*).

A week later, the newspaper published a heavily obscured photo of two of the men allegedly involved, with the caption "Music Figure A and Player A".

Some bloggers and websites later tracked down what they believed to be the original, unobscured image, which showed Cole together with a dance music DJ.

Cole sued the NoW and won the landmark legal argument that he became identified as one of the footballers in their allegations when their article was read alongside material on the web. It was sufficient for Cole to say: "People think it's me."

(BAILII, 2006, EWHC 90070).

Case Study

In 2019, care home manager Kim Suttle was awarded damages of £55,000 by Justice Nicklin following a Facebook 'hate campaign' in which she was accused of abusing a dog.

The court ordered self-declared animal lover Samantha Walker, who ran an anonymous Facebook page called "Justice For Animals Brutally Abused UK", which was likened to a vigilante group, to pay Ms Suttle £55,000 in damages.

As a result of the postings, Ms Suttle had to change her job, and received death threats and threatening phone calls.

Ms Suttle's solicitors, Brett Wilson, went to court to obtain a 'Norwich Pharmacal' order to force Facebook to reveal who was behind the website.

The judge in the case said that "hiding behind anonymity is a hallmark of cyberbullying" (Inforrm, 2019, *Case Law: Suttle v Walker, Facebook 'Keyboard Warrior' Ordered to Pay £55,000 Libel and Harassment Damages*).

(BAILII, 2019, EWHC 396 (QB).)

3. **Publication:** that the words were published to at least one third party. Publication triggers a libel action, and every fresh publication can be treated as a new, separate libel action.

It is not safe for someone to claim that they are merely repeating a libellous statement made by someone else. If they publish it, they are legally responsible for it.

However, web editors who republish their own articles are protected by the DA 2013 if they:

- Provide a new link to their own archived story.

- Repeat one of their old broadcasts.

- Republish an old article because new developments have made it current again.

- Repeat the link or the story via Twitter, email or other social media.

- Publish the article in a new edition of a book.

The DA only covers publishers who republish something they have previously published, provided it does not significantly differ from the original.

It does not protect someone else who publishes the offending material for the first time.

What Is the Time Limit?

Libel actions must be started within 12 months of the date of first publication.

In the online environment, this starts when an article is first published online and is not considered a new publication each time an article is viewed or downloaded unless it is substantially altered or updated.

Where Can a Libel Claimant Start an Action?

Libel tourism used to be a problem in England and Wales because people from overseas took advantage of the strict libel laws and started actions for allegations made on websites in other countries.

They claimed that it was acceptable to use the court in London because the defamatory statements could be viewed in the UK.

However, the DA 2013 tightened this loophole.

Now, someone from outside Europe cannot bring a libel case in London, unless they can prove that England is the most appropriate place for it to be heard and that they have a reputation to defend in England.

So far, Libel tourism has only been considered in one court case under the DA 2013.

(BAILII, 2015, EWHC 3380.)

Mr Justice Tugendhat used it to lay out criteria for when the court will accept cases in England and Wales.

Courts will consider:

- The proportion of times that the article was published in England and Wales as opposed to elsewhere.

- The amount of damage to the claimant's reputation in England and Wales compared with elsewhere.

- The extent to which the publication was targeted at a readership in England and Wales compared with elsewhere.

- Whether there was reason to think that the claimant would not receive a fair hearing elsewhere.

- The convenience of witnesses and the relative expense of suing in different jurisdictions.

The Key Question on Libel

The key issue for web publishers is not whether people *can* sue, but whether they *will* sue.

Publishers will usually weigh up the likelihood of a libel action when deciding whether to publish a contentious story.

It is not uncommon for editors to ask their accounts departments to do credit checks on possible libel claimants to see if they can afford to start proceedings!

Why People Start Libel Actions

- To clear their names.

- To scare off other media and take control of the story.

- To make money.

- Because not acting will make them look guilty.

- To discourage the media from publishing negative stories about them in the future.

Why People Do Not Start Libel Actions

- They cannot afford to.

- They are untroubled by the allegations: some people revel in notoriety.

- The claim is true.

- They fear a publisher may produce unsavoury evidence about them as part of their defence in a court case.

- The risk of perjury: if a claimant denies a truthful allegation under oath, they could face criminal prosecution. This is what happened to the former MP Jonathan Aitken.
  (The Guardian, 1999, *Aitken Jailed for 18 Months.*)

- They do not want the publicity and resulting pressure.

The Dangers of Email

It is possible to defame someone in an email message if it is sent to more than one person – even by mistake.

Content writers should check that they do not accidentally enter email addresses of those who should not receive the email.

This can happen with autocomplete and the 'reply to all' options. This could also breach privacy restrictions under the GDPR.

There is also a danger if, for example, a journalist or researcher emails allegations to another party, for their comment. This technically amounts to publishing them to a third party.

It is important to check emails before forwarding them to other people and make sure that any earlier conversations that could contain defamatory or confidential content are deleted.

Case Study

The dangers of libelling someone in an email message were illustrated in January 2015, when a prominent member of the British Hindu community was awarded £45,000 in damages over two defamatory messages.

In April 2013, Hindu priest Pandit Dr Raj Sharma emailed defamatory allegations about Satish Sharma, general secretary of the National Council of Hindu Temples UK.

The messages were sent to several Hindu temples, MPs and Lords.

Judge Moloney described the allegations as "poison" and said that the email messages percolated way beyond the initial recipients.

(Informm, 2015, *News: Prominent British Hindu Wins £45,000 Damages over Hindu Priest's Defamatory Emails.*)

(BAILII, 2014, EWHC 3349 (QB).)

(Informm, 2015, *Sharma v Sharma Approved Judgment.*)

Libel Defences

Several defences are available to the online publisher, as well as protection for user-generated content (UGC), which will be discussed later in this chapter. The defences are:

Truth

Publishers will win libel cases if they can prove the 'essential' and/or 'substantial' truth of the offending words.

This is more difficult than it sounds. In order to establish that an allegation is substantially true, a publisher may have to provide conclusive evidence such as witness statements, photos, documents, digital data such as text messages, and reports.

There is a big difference between believing that an allegation is true and being able to prove it, on the balance of probability.

Case Study

The Sunday Times was ordered to pay damages to a Conservative MP over sexual misconduct claims, which were repeated in Times Online.

Despite the fact that Daniel Poulter was cleared by an internal panel who found no evidence for the claims, the claims remained online.

(Tobitt, 2019, *Tory MP Wins Libel Payout from Sunday Times over 'Utterly Unfounded' Sex Misconduct Claims.*)

Honest Opinion

This defence applies to:

- Criticisms.

- Observations.

- Remarks.

Honest opinion is a generous defence because it is acceptable to express strong, malicious, spiteful and hurtful views about someone, provided the words are:

Recognisable as comment. Prefacing a statement with 'in my opinion' does not mean that it qualifies as a comment.

For example, this is not a comment:

> Premier League referee Mario Broccoli is not qualified to take charge of top-of-the-table clashes.

Why? Because it suggests he has not passed the relevant refereeing exams – a factual allegation.

This statement, however, would count as comment:

> Premier League referee Mario Broccoli is useless –
> the worse referee to ever walk onto a football
> pitch. He should retire.

It can sometimes be hard to distinguish between a comment and a statement of fact.

The simplest test is that a fact can be proved to be true or false, whereas a comment cannot. However, even the courts sometimes find it difficult to separate the two.

An honestly held view. The writer genuinely held the opinions they expressed.

Based on true facts. The writer should provide the background facts upon which the comment is based, even in general terms.

For example, this statement where the writer is commenting on a long-running public issue would probably be safe:

> **The city council's plan to cut social services spending is disgraceful.** Social services director, Jack Smith, should hang his head in shame. He is an insult to his profession.

The words marked in **bold** indicate the facts on which the writer is commenting.

Privilege

There are certain occasions when the media must be able to publish defamatory content without fear of being sued.

For instance, it would be dangerous for journalists to report court cases or ill-tempered council meetings if their publications could be sued for doing so.

To enable reporting, these occasions are termed 'privileged'.

There are two types of privilege available to the media:

1. **Absolute privilege**. Under the DA 1996, absolute privilege protects media reports of court cases, provided they are fair, accurate, and published contemporaneously with the proceedings held in public.

2. **Qualified privilege.** Under the DA 1952, DA 1996 and DA 2013, qualified privilege protects reports based on:

    - Proceedings at council meetings.

    - Official statements made on behalf of organisations such as local authorities, the police and government departments, and disciplinary findings by governing bodies.

    - Reports of public meetings and press conferences.

    - Peer-reviewed statements in scientific and academic journals.

- Reports of scientific and academic conferences and related documents.

- Articles based on information provided by public companies.

- Reports of proceedings of governments, international conferences and international court proceedings, anywhere in the world.

To ensure qualified privilege, a report must be fair, accurate, on a matter of public concern or benefit, and published without malice.

Some of the above are also subject to publication on request of a reasonable letter or statement of explanation or contradiction, sometimes referred to as the 'right of reply'.

Central and local government bodies frequently publish press releases about court cases that they have prosecuted, using the protection of qualified privilege.

However, some press offices are content to publish press releases that are unbalanced and one-sided, and which contain additional quotes without indicating that they were not part of the court proceedings – a practice that carries its own legal risks.

Some experts take the view that these 'press releases' may actually count as 'court reports' under the DA and should, therefore, be balanced.

Section 1 of the DA says that absolute and qualified privilege protects the 'author' of a court report. But the author does not have to be a journalist. It could be a member of a central or local government media team.

It can also be argued that media teams fulfil the function of 'editors' under DA because they have "[…] editorial or equivalent responsibility for the content of the statement or the decision to publish it" (GOV.UK, 2013, *Defamation Act*).

Tim Crook, Professor in Media and Communications at Goldsmiths, University of London, believes that government press officers risk claims of malice if their press releases are excessively biased and one-sided.

This occurred in the case of Lillie & Reed v Newcastle City Council & Others. Mr Justice Eady found malice in a council media release and awarded the claimants £200,000 each.

(BAILII, 2002, EWHC 1600.)

Prof Crook said: "Privilege can break down as a defence if malice is proved, and if the fairness and accuracy of the reporting / representation is invalidated.

"Public authorities need to be very careful about media releases from court proceedings and legal matters. If malice is proved their qualified privilege crumbles.

"The demise of qualified and experienced court reporters means that so much online journalism is dependent on public authorities publishing media releases on the outcome of court cases.

"Their accounts would, in my opinion, be entitled to qualified privilege, and mainstream professional media publishers should always attribute and source this coverage with caution" (Thom, 2016, *When Government Press Officers Think They Are Court Reporters Justice Could Be the Loser*).

In another case, Ipso ruled that the Hackney Gazette was right to use information supplied to it in a press release about a court case, despite the information being wrong.

The issue was about accepted evidence in the case, which the police later agreed was incorrect.

But Ipso ruled that publication by the newspaper was not a breach of clause 1 (accuracy) because the article was accurately based on the official police press release.

(HoldtheFrontPage, 2019, *Weekly Entitled to Rely on Inaccurate Police Press Release, Rules Ipso.*)

Some will say that this practice of publishing one-sided court reports seems to go against natural justice. People prosecuted by a government body may not receive balanced media coverage unless there's a 'real' journalist or blogger in court.

It also invites the question: why do government media teams, who so frequently complain about press bias, choose not to cover both sides of a story, especially when there is a legal argument for doing so?

Many experts would take the view that a court report is too important to be subjected to the 'spin' process.

Case Study

In June 2019, the High Court ruled that a press office is not responsible for libel created by inaccuracy or spin, which alters the meaning of what they have said.

In the case of Alsaifi v Secretary of State for Education, the judge Anthony Metzer said in his judgment, that a press office is only responsible for the wording of a quote. It is not responsible for any errors or misleading aspects of the context in which it appears.

He said: "The source cannot be held responsible for inaccuracy, spin or additional material added by the media publisher which alters the meaning of the source material to make it defamatory" (BAILII, 2019, EWHC 1413, (QB)).

Public Interest

Under the DA 2013, the public interest defence can be used if a publisher has a 'reasonable belief' that publishing a defamatory allegation is in the public interest.

Publishers will have to demonstrate that the copy was balanced and neutral and that thorough steps had been taken to verify the facts.

The DA 2013's explanatory notes say that this defence is intended to reflect the law as set out in Flood v Times Newspapers (2012).

In his judgment, Lord Mance stated that it would seldom be in the public interest "[…] to publish material which has not been the subject of responsible journalistic enquiry and consideration […]" (BAILII, 2012, UKSC 11).

Case Study

The case of Economou v de Freitas was the first example to examine the defence in detail.

It clarified that the court will place a great deal of weight on whether the defendant 'reasonably believed' that the publication was in the public interest, and not just on whether it was a general matter of public interest.

(EWHC, 2016, 1853 (QB).)

The defendant (D) was the father of the late Eleanor de Freitas. In December 2012, Ms de Freitas and the claimant (C) had a relationship.

She accused him of rape the following year, and C was later arrested and charged. Ms de Freitas denied the charge and committed suicide four days before the trial date.

D wanted the subsequent inquest to examine the Crown Prosecution Service's role in this. The coroner initially ruled against this, and D was advised by his solicitor to go public with a series of media statements and broadcasts, which he did in November and December 2014.

C then sued The Guardian, BBC Radio 4 Today, The Daily Telegraph and The Guardian for libel.

D successfully used the public interest defence, with Mr Justice Warby saying that the defence depended on the specific circumstances of each case.

In this case, there was a distinction between the defendant, as the father who had lost a child, and a journalist, whose reasons for pursuing publication would be different.

In 2018, the case was heard at the Court of Appeal and the decision of Mr Justice Warby on the correct use of the public interest defence was upheld.

The appeal court said that, in accordance with the previous Reynolds defence, D had taken several responsible steps with regard to publication.

These included having first-hand knowledge of the history of the case, avoiding naming the defendant, and adopting a measured tone in publication.

The fact that the 'target' of his allegations was a public body, the CPS, rather than the claimant, was also taken into account.

(BAILLI, EWCA, 2591, 2018.)

Case Study

Further direction on the public interest defence was given in a ruling by the Court of Appeal in which a Polish builder claimed to have been subjected to a "character assassination" by a magazine.

The allegations concerned cheating and profiting from a care home and a jazz club he was connected to, allegations which, according to Justice Jay, the magazine had a public interest in airing.

Legal website Inforrm says that the case gives clarity for publishers to the section 4 defence under the 2013 DA.

(Inforrm, 2019, *Case Law: Serafin v Malkiewicz, Public Interest Defence Considered Again, and Judicial Unfairness*.)

(Courts and Tribunals Judiciary, 2017, EWHC 2992 (QB).)

Bane and Antidote

Publishers can sometimes call upon what is known as the 'bane and antidote' defence.

This is where an apparently libellous headline has the sting taken out of it by the 'antidote' in either a subhead or the main copy.

A recent example involved a defamatory headline and two defendants charged in connection with the death of a young woman following a road race.

Action was taken over the headline on the Metropolitan Police's own website: "Two guilty of killing a woman while racing their cars."

Both drivers had been arrested and charged with causing death and causing injury by dangerous driving, but only one was convicted on both of the charges at crown court.

Mr Justice Warby said that the headline had to be read in the context with the rest of the article, which made it clear who was directly responsible for the death.

This kind of case shows the leeway editors have in writing more contentious headlines.

(BAILII, 2019, EWHC, QB, 1439.)

How to Protect Copy from Libel

Anyone who publishes online or on social media should always:

- Check their facts and only write statements where the meaning is clear, and which can be proved to be true, with solid, reliable evidence. They should take care that words used for effect in headlines and introductions are supported by evidence – for example, the word 'shameful'.

  Inferences and barbed remarks must be proved as well.

- Tweets pose a particular danger because of their brevity and their potential for being misread. The law takes account of what the ordinary person reads into a tweet, not what the author meant by it.

- Check that sources are credible and willing to appear as witnesses in a libel trial.

- Corroborate allegations. Single-source allegations should be treated with caution.

- Exercise sufficient care and judgment in researching, compiling and presenting their stories.

  They should mention what information they do not know, so that readers understand the broader picture.

- Avoid words that deal with motives; for example, 'misleading' or 'deliberately'.

- Check which defence the claimant would use if the case went to court, and make sure that they can comply with the conditions.

Libel on Twitter (Twibel)

It is safe for online publishers or bloggers to tweet or retweet comments if they fulfil the conditions of the honest opinion defence, outlined above.

However, tweets or retweets can be defamatory, if they contain a factual allegation that causes, or is likely to cause, serious harm to someone's reputation.

Case Study

The best example of a 'Twibel' was the case of Lord McAlpine v Sally Bercow.

Two days after a Newsnight report that wrongly implicated the former Conservative party treasurer in allegations of historic sex abuse, Bercow posted a tweet saying: "Why is Lord McAlpine trending? *Innocent face*" (Carruthers Law, 2013, *Lord McAlpine of West Green v Sally Bercow*).

McAlpine said it pointed the finger of blame, and he won undisclosed damages.

Bercow did not actually make an allegation against the peer. She just made a pointed suggestion that was seen as libel by innuendo, as it contained a hidden meaning.

(BAILII, 2013, EWHC 1342 (QB).)

Case Study

In 2018, Bristol's UKIP branch chairman Steve Wood had £40,000 in damages awarded against him after a tweet was sent out by his agent on his (Wood's) Twitter account.

Wood never saw or sanctioned the tweet but had delegated the posting of tweets to his vice-chair John Langley, with instructions not to post racist or defamatory tweets.

Labour party member Zahir Monir sued for defamation after he was featured in a tweet sent out by Langley – Wood's agent during the 2015 general election – containing child abuse allegations.

Mr Justice Nicklin said that Mr Monir had been "seriously libelled" in the post (BAILLI, 2018, EWHC 3525).

How to Make Tweets and Retweets Safe from Libel

Anyone who publishes on Twitter should always:

- Check copy and headings for hidden meanings.

- Check the facts can be proved – even in retweets.

- Review hashtags. For example, this is safe (if it is true):

  BBC reports that England star Barry Briggs was stopped for speeding.

But these hashtags make the statement potentially defamatory:

> BBC reports that England star Barry Briggs was stopped for speeding #dangerous #driver #criminal.

Libel on Facebook

It is also possible to libel someone on Facebook.

Case Study

A case heard at the Supreme Court in 2019 illustrates an interesting development in how the law views libel on social media.

In 2012, in a Facebook exchange with her ex-husband's new partner, Nicola Stocker alleged that her then-husband Nigel Stocker had "tried to strangle" her and made other threats to her.

Mr Stocker sued for libel, claiming that that the post meant he had tried to kill his ex-wife. She claimed that the words merely meant he had grabbed her by the throat.

Mr Stocker won his case, with the judge – after consulting the Oxford English Dictionary – deciding that the meaning of "to kill" was conveyed in the words.

An appeal by Mrs Stocker failed and the case was subsequently heard before five judges at the Supreme Court.

They allowed the appeal, saying the judge should not have consulted a dictionary for a meaning of words and that the context of the allegations on Facebook had to be taken into account.

The Supreme Court said the law should take into account what an "ordinary reasonable reader" would take the words to mean, especially when they are posted on social media.

In their judgment, the judges stated: "The fact that this was a Facebook post is critical" and that the way people post and read comments on Facebook must be taken into account.

Tellingly, the judges said that social media is a "casual medium", where "people scroll through Facebook quickly and their reaction to posts is impressionistic and fleeting".

They stated: "An ordinary reader of the post would have interpreted the post as meaning that Mr Stocker had grasped Mrs Stocker by the throat and applied force to her neck."

The consequences of this judgment seem to be that there is a higher threshold for libel on social media.

(BAILII, 2019, UKSC 17.)

Libel on Message Boards

The lesson for media running unmoderated message boards is clear.

They have immunity from prosecution under the EU ECD Regulations, but that immunity may fail if they do not respond quickly to take-down requests about posts that involve breaches of the law.

Three laws currently provide publishers with defences for legal actions resulting from posts on their message boards:

- EU ECD Regulations 2002.

- DA 1996: section 1.

- DA 2013: section 5. This defence requires a lot of complex administration, and it is hard to see why a web editor would use it.

These laws are alike and state that online publishers are not responsible for online visitors' posts, if:

- **They do not moderate the content**: their message boards are just a means of storing and passing on information and are not edited.

  The following actions can be interpreted as editing:

  o Manually updating entries on a homepage's auto-generated lists of blogs and recommended blogs.

  o Correcting spelling and grammar.

  o Controlling quality.

  o Deleting spam.

  o Deleting obscenity, bad language, etc.

- **They operate a 'report and remove' system:** they take down offensive posts promptly if they receive a complaint.

Case Study

The ECtHR has also examined the publication of readers' comments.

In the case Magyar Tartalomszolgaltatok Egyesulete and Index.Hu Zrt v Hungary, the ECtHR ruled, in February 2016, that making websites responsible for the content of the comments section would breach freedom of expression rights.

The case involved a Hungarian website that was sued for messages on its forum about a company. The comments were removed as soon as they were reported.

Defence lawyers said there would be serious repercussions on freedom of expression if their clients were liable for everything that readers posted.

The judges agreed and ruled that Hungarian courts were wrong to rule in favour of the unnamed company.

They said in their judgment: "Although offensive and vulgar, the incriminated comments did not constitute clearly unlawful speech; and they certainly did not amount to hate speech or incitement to violence" (BAILII, 2016, ECHR 135).

Case Study

The system of 'report and remove' was thrown into some doubt by a surprising decision by the ECtHR.

The case involved the large Estonian news website, Delfi, in 2015.

In January 2006, Delfi published a story about a ferry company's controversial decision to change its routes.

The article attracted more than 180 comments, including 20 that threatened and abused the ferry company's majority shareholder.

The comments bypassed Delfi's automatic 'bad language' filters.

The ferry company sued for libel and won both its case and an appeal under Estonian libel law, even though Delfi removed the comments quickly after receiving a complaint.

Delfi took the case to the ECtHR, claiming that the Estonian courts breached their rights of freedom of expression.

However, the court found in favour of the ferry company's majority shareholder, and Delfi was fined €320.

The judges said: "By publishing the article in question, [Delfi] could have realised that it might cause negative reactions against the shipping company and its managers and that, considering the general reputation of comments on the Delfi news portal, there was a higher-than-average risk that the negative comments could go beyond the boundaries of acceptable criticism and reach the level of gratuitous insult or hate speech" (BAILII, ECHR 941, 2013).

This ruling appeared to contradict the ECD and showed that there are some circumstances when 'report and remove' cannot be relied upon.

Delfi appealed the decision and in June 2015 the Grand Chamber of the European Court supported the ECtHR's earlier decision by a majority of 15-2.

It agreed that Delfi was liable for making the 'grossly insulting' comments available on its website and that the company exercised a substantial degree of control over its news portal.

The judges said that Delfi's role went beyond that of a passive, purely technical service provider.

(BAILII, ECHR 586, 2015.)

However, as is often the case with online media law, another case in the same court has thrown the Delfi decision itself into doubt.

The court upheld the decision of a Norwegian court in a libel case brought by a lawyer – over posts made in a discussion forum on a news website – not to award damages or find the website liable.

The ECtHR said that the alleged defamatory comments could not be counted as the editorial product of the site, Hegnar Online, and ruled that the discussion forum had to be viewed separately.

In addition, the court said that the comments about the lawyer, while hurtful, did not directly affect her reputation.

(BAILLI, 2019, ECHR, 221.)

Although this ruling seems to contradict that of the case above, it should be remembered that the comments on the Delfi site amounted to hate speech.

It remains to be seen what effect this ruling, and the appeal, will have on UK websites.

UK courts are not legally bound by ECtHR decisions. They must only "take them into account". However, they generally attempt to make judgments that are compatible with the convention.

The European Commission (EC) began a review of the ECD in 2015.

It was published in 2018 and, among other things, examined the liability of hosting companies like Facebook and Twitter for content on their platforms.

The EC has published a proposed Digital Content Directive that will tighten the rules on hosting liability, but this is unlikely to come into effect until 2020.

However, the government has identified it as a possible area where UK law could diverge from that of the EU.

CHAPTER 3

CONTEMPT OF COURT

Anyone who publishes online can face criminal prosecution if they publish something that could influence a jury.

Case Study

In the past, it was mainly journalists who risked prosecution under contempt of court legislation.

However, the conviction of the ex-English Defence League leader Tommy Robinson (real name Stephen Yaxley-Lennon), in July 2019, shows that anyone who broadcasts online using Facebook Live or similar channels needs to exercise caution.

Robinson was originally jailed for 13 months for contempt on the day of the Facebook broadcast but was released two months into his sentence after winning an appeal.

However, the Attorney General (AG) reviewed the case and said it was in the public interest to bring fresh proceedings.

Robinson was jailed for nine months for contempt of court, reduced to 19 weeks after time spent in custody was taken into account.

Mr Cox said after the trial: "I would urge everyone to think carefully about whether their social media posts could amount to contempt of court" (BAILII, 2019, EWHC 1791 (QB)).

Case Study

A trial at crown court was abandoned by the judge after a comment was posted about the case on a newspaper's website.

The Newsquest regional newspaper – which was not named – was referred to the AG in September 2018 following the comment posted while the case was active.

In a memo to staff, Newsquest editorial director Toby Granville said: "In circumstances like this there could be a prosecution under the Contempt of Court Act as well as statutory power under the Courts Act 2003 that allows the courts to recover wasted costs of retrial from a third party where the 'serious conduct' of that third party affects a case."

He reminded staff to disable online comments for live court cases.

(HoldtheFrontPage.co.uk, 2018, *Judge Abandons Crown Court Trial Due to Comment on Regional Press Story.*)

Case Study

In 2012, while the jury was considering its verdict in the case of the alleged abduction of a teenage girl (Rachel Cowles), the Daily Mirror and the Daily Mail published an allegation that the defendant, Levi Bellfield, had a sexual interest in young girls.

The newspapers published the allegation after a jury had found Bellfield guilty of the kidnap and murder of teenager Milly Dowler, but before it had reached a verdict in relation to the kidnap attempt on Rachel.

The court fined the newspapers for publishing prejudicial material. This contempt of court was so serious that the jury was discharged.

(BAILII, 2012, EWHC 2981.)

The Contempt of Court Act (CoCA) 1981's strict liability rule says that any publication that creates a substantial risk of serious prejudice or impediment to the administration of justice may be treated as contempt, regardless of intent, if proceedings are active.

'Active' usually covers the period from someone's arrest to the conclusion of their trial.

(CPS, 2009, Contempt of Court and Reporting Restrictions: Strict Liability Contempt under the Contempt of Court Act 1981.)

However, in June 2019, it emerged that the government had extended the scope of active proceedings. This development is likely to hinder reporting.

In the past, proceedings following an arrest only deactivated when:

- The suspect was released (unless on police bail).

- The suspect was charged.

These both still apply.

Now, however, if someone is arrested, proceedings will remain active if someone is released while under police investigation.

And they will remain active until the police custody officer tells the suspect in writing that the investigation is no longer being continued.

This means that media coverage in these circumstances may be restricted for long periods.

A Home Office spokesman told the Press Gazette in June: "Journalists can still make inquiries to the police in such cases, as they would have previously in investigations where suspects were released on bail"(*PA Media Lawyer, 2019, Contempt risk remains for released suspects still 'under investigation' by police after law change*).

The new law was introduced after the Policing and Crime Act 2017 limited police bail to 28 days, following complaints that it sometimes dragged on for long periods.

Police now release people 'under investigation', instead.

CoCA was amended by the Policing and Crime Act 2017 (Consequential Amendments) Regulations 2018 (2018 No. 226).

What Does CoCA Apply To?

The Act says that any writing, speech, broadcast or other communication can be in contempt, so anyone who publishes online or on social media needs to check their content carefully.

Former AG Dominic Grieve said he would prosecute publishers of social media remarks that breached the law. Legal warnings are posted on the AG's Twitter feed @attorneygeneral, and its website.

The risks of prejudice increase if:

- A trial is less than six months away; the nearer it gets, the greater the risk.

- It is a high-profile or memorable case that sticks in jurors' minds.

- A trial is in progress.

Content that Can Create Prejudice

The main dangers are:

- Suggesting that the person who was arrested is the same person who committed the crime, or using details that imply it, for example: 'The suspect was arrested carrying a sawn-off shotgun.'

- Commenting on the credibility of witnesses or their evidence.

- Saying why a defendant might be guilty or innocent.

- Revealing a defendant's previous convictions or their acquittals.

- Mentioning details of a defendant's lifestyle, character or previous court appearances.

- Publishing descriptions or photos of the defendant, especially if they are basing their defence on mistaken identity.

  This applies unless photos, photofits or detailed descriptions are used as part of a police appeal to apprehend a suspected criminal.

  However, they should not continue to be used once a defendant has been arrested.

- Disclosing information that the jury has not yet heard.

- Publishing links to pre-trial stories.

- Mentioning cases involving a defendant.

The AG, the police, or counsel involved in the case can ask webmasters to remove online material that could create prejudice.

They can also apply to the court for a CoCA section 4 order to delay the publication of prejudicial material, until a date set by the court. See the section Defences, below.

Case Study

In February 2016, the Court of Appeal made an order, under section 45(4) of the Senior Courts Act 1981, against a group of nine media organisations, forbidding them to publish reports of a trial on their Facebook profiles and pages.

It also told them to disable their website message boards.

The trial was of a case of two girls charged with the murder of Angela Wrightson, 39, who was battered to death in her home in Hartlepool in December 2014.

A previous trial of this case was halted at Teesside Crown Court in July 2015, following a wave of comment and abuse on social media.

Editors were warned that they may face prosecution under the CoCA, if they did not comply with the order.

This was the first time the Court of Appeal issued a specific ban on social media, to prevent comments from prejudicing a trial.

In a similar move in April 2016, media organisations covering the trial of two women accused of murdering a two-year-old were asked not to publish stories on social media, and to disable their message boards.

The Scottish Courts and Tribunals Service made the request because potentially prejudicial comments were being posted under reports of the trial of Nyomi Fee, 28, and Rachel Fee, 31, for the murder of Rachel's son Liam in a house near Glenrothes in March 2014.

As illustrated by the Newsquest example above, web editors should not allow people to comment on crimes or court cases once proceedings are active.

Archived material is usually safe, provided the website does not provide a new link to it, draw attention to it, or republish it.

However, web editors need to make sure that automatic tools do not produce unwanted links to active cases.

(HoldtheFrontPage, 2016, *Wrightson Judge Explains Why He Kept Killers' Names Secret*.)

Case Study

In 2016, the Lancashire newspaper St Helens Star asked readers to refrain from commenting on a Facebook social signal about an ongoing court case involving local MP Marie Rimmer.

However, the newspaper's followers quickly weighed in with comments ranging from the MP being as "guilty as hell" to "Marie didn't do anything wrong."

One follower probably struck a more helpful note by stating: "Why not just turn the option off to post comments then?"

Ms Rimmer was later acquitted of kicking a Yes campaigner outside a polling station in Scotland on the day of the Scottish independence referendum.

(Facebook, 2016, *Campaigner Tells Court She Did Not Provoke Alleged Kick.*)

(Carrell, 2016, *Labour MP Cleared of Kicking Scottish Independence Campaigner*.)

In addition, it is now common for the police to advise victims of crime and their families to avoid any online comments that could help suspects to argue that they cannot get a fair trial.

Other Contempt of Court Risks

It is also possible to commit contempt of court by:

- Naming or identifying jurors.

- Disclosing, obtaining or soliciting information about statements made, opinions expressed, arguments advanced, or votes cast by members of a jury.

These actions are crimes under section 74 of the Criminal Justice and Courts Act 2015.

A person could be jailed for up to two years, or given an unlimited fine, if convicted of the crimes.

(UK Legislation, n.d., *Criminal Justice and Courts Act 2015*.)

- Breaching a court injunction. Some people's identities are protected by a lifelong injunction.

  The best-known example of a 'blanket injunction' is Maxine Carr, who provided a false alibi for her boyfriend Ian Huntley, after he murdered Holly Wells and Jessica Chapman, in Soham, Cambridgeshire in 2002.

Case Study

An 18-year-old youth – referred to only as RXG – was granted lifelong anonymity in 2019 after a trial in which he was found guilty of inciting terrorism abroad.

The youth, from Blackburn, carried out the offences when he was 14 and is the youngest person in the UK to be convicted of terror offences.

Reporting restrictions imposed at the time of his trial gave him anonymity but this was extended by the courts when he was approaching his 18th birthday.

The High Court heard that the defendant suffered from autism and could be subject to attack if his identity was known.

Mr Justice Nicklin said the youth's case was "exceptional" and that loss of his anonymity posed a threat "in terms of his rehabilitation and reintegration to society when released" (BAILII, 2019, EWHC 2026 (QB)).

Case Study

Robert Thompson and Jon Venables who, as children, were convicted of murdering James Bulger, have their new identities protected by an injunction.

However, in March 2019, Hollyoaks and Shameless actress Tina Malone was ordered to pay £10,000 costs by the High Court and given an eight-month suspended sentence after sharing a Facebook post revealing Venables' new name, together with a current image of him.

Malone, who was found guilty of contempt in breaching the anonymity order, told the court she did not realise that sharing the post amounted to a criminal offence.

(BBC News, 2019, *Tina Malone Admits 'Bulger Killer Photo' Facebook Post.*)

Two defendants were given similar suspended jail sentences for publishing information about Venables and Thompson in breach of the same order.

In a separate case, Richard McKeag and Natalie Barker both admitted contempt, McKeag being sentenced to 12 months, and Barker to eight months, both suspended for two years.

(Courts and Tribunals Judiciary, 2019, *Committals for Contempt of Court at the Royal Courts of Justice: McKeag, Barker.*)

Case Study

In December 2016, the High Court passed a lifelong injunction on two brothers who tortured two children in South Yorkshire when they were aged 10 and 11.

They were originally granted anonymity until the age of 18, in 2010. The High Court extended the anonymity because they would be at serious risk of attack.

The boys lured their victims to a ravine and carried out a "sadistic" attack in Edlington, near Doncaster, in 2009.

(BBC News, 2010, *Edlington Attack 'Could Have Been Prevented'.*)

(BAILII, 2016, EWHC 3295 (Ch).)

Defences

The CoCA provides three defences for contempt by publication:

1. **Innocent publication**. Under section 3 of the CoCA, online publishers may have the defence of innocent publication if they can prove that having taken all reasonable care, they did not know and had no reason to believe that proceedings were active.

    This means that online publishers must check if proceedings are active in a case, which may involve checking with the police (or press officer) and with the court before they publish or upload their stories.

Details of the time and date of the call, the name of the officer or official spoken to, and the nature of their reply should be noted in writing.

This defence also applies to the new 'under investigation' arrangements mentioned above.

But in reality, it is likely to be difficult to use if, for example, an investigation continues for weeks or even months. It is hardly practical for journalists to call the press office every few days to check the situation.

The best advice is for them to err on the side of caution, if they cannot establish the latest position.

2. **Contemporary reports of proceedings**. Under the section 4 defence of the CoCA the media will not be liable for publishing a court report that prejudices another case, provided the report is:

- Fair.

- Accurate.

- Published contemporaneously.

- Published in good faith.

However, a judge may override the section 4 defence by passing a section 4 order, as mentioned above, which will delay the publication of a report of a case (or some other material, like a photo) until a given date.

When judges pass the section 4 order, they must state:

- Why it was passed.

- The evidence it applies to.

- When it expires.

3. **Discussion in good faith of public affairs**. The CoCA's section 5 defence allows the media to publish background stories about issues arising from a court case, but not the case itself, while proceedings are active, provided they are in the public interest and the risk of prejudice is incidental to the discussion.

   For example, if a teenager is arrested today for stabbing a fellow pupil at school, proceedings will be active.

   However, it would be safe for the media to publish stories (accompanying the newsbreak), on subjects such as security in schools and the availability of knives on the internet.

   This defence may provide the media with a way of getting around the new 'under investigation' arrangements mentioned above.

   We may see a proliferation of 'backgrounders', while investigations into an arrested suspect continue.

Protecting People's Identities

Anyone who publishes online can be prosecuted for contempt of court if they upload content or images that identify someone who is legally protected, including:

- Alleged victims of any sexual offence, or victims of alleged Female Genital Mutilation (FGM) and forced marriage.

- Under-18s involved in crime, either as suspects, defendants, witnesses or victims.

- Teachers accused of offences against pupils at their schools.

- Under-18s, and certain adults, involved in ward of court or family court cases.

The law is applied strictly. People with protected identities must remain anonymous, even to people who know them, including their parents, partners, husbands, wives, and close family members or work colleagues.

The more details that are used, the more dangerous it is, especially when facts are used together with a person's age. Ages are best generalised.

It is also important to check which details other media have used, to avoid the 'jigsaw effect'. Web editors should just use the same details and not add any other facts.

Media organisations should make sure that they use the same details in items appearing on their printed, web, and social media platforms.

However, if an online visitor reveals someone's identity on an unmoderated media website, the web editor may be safe from prosecution under the EU ECD.

Risks with Photos

Photos should be checked, even if they have been pixelated because they might include identifying features such as hairstyles, hats or clothes and tattoos. A location can also provide clues, so these must be checked.

Photos of people facing away from the camera or taken from behind should also be checked, in case they lead to identification.

Case Study

In March 2016, ex-Sun newspaper editor David Dinsmore was ordered to pay £2,300 in costs and compensation for breaching the Sexual Offences (Amendment) Act 1992 for publishing a photo of a sexual offence victim.

The Sun printed a Facebook photo of a teenage girl who had fallen victim to former AFC Sunderland player, Adam Johnson, who was subsequently jailed for grooming and sexual activity with a child.

The newspaper took extensive steps to obscure the girl's identity: it replaced the background, changed the girl's clothing, the length and colour of her hair, and substituted her head with an oval white shape.

However, Westminster Magistrates Court ruled that people who had seen the Facebook page would realise that the Sun had used the same image.

They used the strict legal test: could she be identified as a victim by people who knew her?

The Sun had mistakenly used a lower threshold: could she be identified by the average man and woman in the street?

This was surprising, as the stricter test had been widely used for many years.

The case indicates the lengths to which the courts will go to safeguard people whose identities are legally protected.

(Perraudin, 2016, *Former Sun Editor Convicted over Adam Johnson Victim Picture.*)

Risks with Written Content

Facts that can lead to identification must be removed, especially when used with a location such as the name of a village or small geographical area, or a geotag that includes a postcode.

Other facts that need to be checked include:

Unusual details about a person

For example:

- She has eight brothers and sisters.
- He rides a quad bike.
- Her mother is a ballet teacher.
- She was out walking her two Dalmatians.

The circumstances of a crime

For example:

- She was on her way home from her French evening class.

- It happened in Victoria Park, just after the under-12s cup final.

- He was following his usual journey to work after catching the 8.10am from London Bridge.

Specific details of injuries sustained in an attack

For example:

- She received 50 stitches to a facial wound.

- He is now on crutches.

- Her hands were seriously burned in the attack.

Cases involving people from the same family

These must be treated with extreme care; for instance, if a father is accused of indecently assaulting his child.

Clause 7 of the Ipso Editors' Code of Practice specifies that:

- The child must not be identified.

- The adult may be identified.

- The word 'incest' must not be used where a child victim might be identified.

Care must be taken that nothing in the report implies the relationship between the accused and the child.

This may mean that many significant details of the case, including much of the evidence, must be omitted.

When Anonymity Applies

These are the main circumstances when anonymity applies.

Alleged Sexual Offences

The Sexual Offences Act (SOA) 2003, when taken with the Sexual Offences Act 1976 and the Criminal Justice Act (CJA) 1988, says that a complainant of any sexual offence may not be identified as an alleged victim, in their lifetime, from the moment of complaint.

The Youth Justice and Criminal Evidence Act (YJCEA) 1999 forbids the use of:

- Their name, address, school, college or workplace.

- Any particulars leading to their identification.

- Any photo of or including them.

These restrictions apply to all online and social media publishers, including individuals.

In addition, Ipso's Editors' Code of Practice was updated in 2019 to tighten reporting around sex offences and to further protect the identity of victims.

Clause 11 (Victims of sexual assault) was revised after complaints were received about potential identification breaches by the media.

A new addition to the clause reads: "Journalists are entitled to make enquiries but must take care and exercise discretion to avoid the unjustified disclosure of the identity of a victim of sexual assault" (Ipso, 2019, *Editors' Code of Practice*.)

It followed cases involving the Sun and the Daily Mail, which both made enquiries among family or friends that could have identified a victim of a sex offence.

It cannot be assumed that even close family are aware of the alleged incident.

Under-18s Involved in Crime

Most court cases involving under-18s are dealt with in youth courts.

However, some young people are tried in an adult magistrates court or the crown court, if they are charged with serious offences or jointly charged with an adult.

When a child or young person appears in a youth court, either as a defendant, witness or a victim, the Children and Young Persons Act 1933 and YJCEA 1999 jointly and automatically forbid the reporting of the same details listed in point 1, above.

On conviction, the media can apply for the restrictions to be lifted in the public interest, under the Crime (Sentences) Act 1997.

The restrictions can also be lifted by the home secretary, under the Children and Young Persons Act 1969, to prevent the possibility of injustice to a juvenile.

In addition, the director of public prosecutions may apply for the lifting under the Criminal Justice and Public Order Act 1994, to trace a juvenile wanted for a violent or sexual offence or any offence for which an adult could be jailed for 14 years or more.

If under-18s appear in an adult court, they can be named, unless the court passes a section 45 order under the YJCEA.

The order can be passed on witnesses, victims and defendants, and the anonymity requirements are the same as above.

These are the key points about section 45 orders:

- Any criminal court can pass the order on any under-18 victim, witness or defendant who is involved in the proceedings.

- The order applies to print and broadcast media and online publications.

- When deciding whether to pass the order, the court must have regard to the welfare of the child or young person.

- If it is passed, the media cannot publish the child's name, address or school, college or workplace, or any particulars leading to their identification by people who know them; or any photo of or including any such juvenile.

- The court may remove or relax the section 45 reporting restriction if satisfied that it imposes a substantial and unreasonable restriction on reporting, and that it is in the public interest.

  This means that the media can challenge the order on these grounds.

- The order expires when the child or young person turns 18, or when proceedings finish if they turn 18 during the case. But a victim or witness may have their anonymity protected for the rest of their lives in certain circumstances.

- The order cannot be passed just because the person is under-18. The court must balance the child's welfare against the public interest and the media's right to report.

- The media can challenge an order by persuading the court that:

  o It imposes a substantial and unreasonable restriction on reporting, and

  o It is in the public interest.

Case Study

In Scotland in 2019, a judge lifted anonymity on 16-year-old child killer Aaron Campbell, jailed for life for the murder of six-year-old Alesha MacPhail on the Isle of Bute.

The judge in the case heard representations from the press that Campbell's identity had been widely known on the internet for many months.

This, combined with the heinous nature of the crime, resulted in Judge Lord Matthews allowing him to be named.

Interestingly, Scottish law has only recently come in line with English law regarding youth anonymity. Until 2015, juvenile defendants could be named on turning 16.

(BBC News, 2019, *Alesha MacPhail Murder: Judge Lifts Ban on Naming Killer Aaron Campbell.*)

Case Study

Press regulator Ipso ruled in favour of the Brighton Argus when it published video footage on its website of teenage girls on a bus threatening to stab rail passengers.

The footage showed the unpixelated faces of the two 15-year-olds making threats to rob passengers on a train.

The mother of one of the girls complained to Ipso that the website had breached clause 2 (privacy) of the code, as well as clause 6 (children).

She said her daughter had received threats after being identified in the report and had not been able to attend school after the Argus had published the footage, which had been posted on Facebook and widely shared.

But Ipso said there was "clear public interest in reporting this potentially criminal activity, in that doing so contributed to an ongoing public debate around young people's involvement in crime" *(Ipso, 2019, 07908-18, A Woman v theargus.co.uk).*

Teacher Anonymity

Teachers accused of offences against children at their schools receive lifelong anonymity under the Education Act (EA) 2011, unless they are charged.

Victims of FGM and Forced Marriage

The media must not identify victims and alleged victims of FGM and related offences, once an allegation has been made.

This provision comes under section 71 of the Serious Crime Act (SCA) 2015, and also covers offences related to FGM.

Victims and alleged victims of forced marriage also receive lifelong anonymity under an amendment to the Anti-social Behaviour, Crime and Policing Act 2014.

Wards of Court Hearings and Family Law Cases

Section 12 of the Administration of Justice Act, and the Children Act 1989 impose strict restrictions on reporting such hearings and on identifying people involved in the cases. It may not be possible to report them at all.

Case Study

Freelance reporter Louise Tickle challenged reporting restrictions in the family courts and won a landmark case at the Court of Appeal over an adoption case.

Tickle and a BBC reporter picked up the story through a Court of Appeal judgment, but the family court judge forbade the media to publish certain details in the case, making it all but impossible to report.

The case went to appeal and was allowed by the president of the family division of the High Court, Sir Andrew McFarlane.

In light of the case, he promised to issue new guidance to courts and the media regarding the challenging of reporting restrictions and access to family court cases.

HMCTS issued draft guidance to courts in May 2019.

Sir Andrew also initiated a consultation on permanent changes which concluded in June 2019.

(Judiciary.co.uk, 2019, *President's Guidance: Guidance as to Reporting in the Family Courts*.)

(Gov.UK, 2019, *New Media Guidance Issued to All Court Staff*.)

COURT REPORTING

Any member of the public, including journalists, bloggers and content writers, may attend and report court cases, subject to a range of restrictions that can be downloaded here:

https://www.judiciary.gov.uk/publications/reporting-restrictions-in-the-criminal-courts-2/

It is contempt of court to make audio recordings of court proceedings.

In addition, the CJA 1925 makes it an offence to take or publish a photo or sketch of parties or witnesses in the courtroom, or of people entering or leaving the court or its precincts.

The term 'precincts' has never been defined, so this can cause uncertainty for media wanting to photograph people involved in court cases.

The safest option is to photograph them away from the court buildings and to heed any instructions from police or court officials to move on.

The media should also make sure that they do not publish photos of jurors or of people whose identities are legally protected.

And they should check that these people are not inadvertently included in background shots.

Tweeting from Court

The lord chief justice said, in 2012, that journalists and legal commentators can cover court cases using Twitter or liveblogging platforms, without consent.

The term 'legal commentators' is seen as applying to bloggers.

Guidance is available on this downloadable pdf:

https://www.judiciary.gov.uk/wp-content/uploads/JCO/Documents/Guidance/ltbc-guidance-dec-2011.pdf

Despite the guidance, it appears that not all courts have got the message. Hunts Post reporter Katie Ridley told HoldtheFrontPage that she was twice asked by a court usher not to use her phone to tweet during a court case.

The judge at Peterborough Crown Court dismissed the usher's concerns but Katie said: "It's becoming frustrating now that journalists seem to get treated so differently, and that a lot of court staff still do not understand journalists' rights" (HoldtheFrontPage, 2019, *Journalist Claims Court Staff Trying to Intimidate Her Because She Is Young and Female'*).

These tweeted reports, when taken together, must be a fair, balanced, and accurate summary. This can be challenging in a series of 280-character tweets.

In cases where a defendant pleads not guilty, journalists and legal commentators should ensure that each day's tweets:

- Include the defendant's plea.

- Do not present allegations as fact. Evidence must be frequently qualified with statements like: 'The jury heard', or 'It was alleged'.

- State that the case continues in the final tweet at the end of each day's proceedings.

Journalists and bloggers are also advised to avoid using hashtags that can lead to other tweets containing prejudicial material or restricted identities.

Taking Notes in Court

It is not unusual for judges and magistrates to challenge note-taking, or even ban it, as they did during the Operation Elveden trials, although this restriction only applied to people in the public gallery, not the press benches.

However, the position should change following a ruling by the Queen's Bench Division (QBD) of the High Court, discussed in the case study below.

The court ruled that anyone (the press or the public) can take notes without consent. However, a court can still ban note-taking, if there is a good reason to do so.

Case Study

The case Ewing v Cardiff Crown Court involved a man called Terence Ewing, who was threatened with contempt after a judge spotted him taking notes in the public gallery during an appeal case in 2014.

Ewing appealed the ruling and won his argument.

The QBD judges, Lord Justice Burnett and Mr Justice Sweeney, said the judge in the original case was wrong.

They referred to HM Courts and Tribunals Service guidelines to staff, which say: "There can be no objection to note-taking in the public gallery, unless it is done for a wrongful purpose; for example, to brief a witness who is not in court on what has already happened" (BAILII, 2016, EWHC 183).

They said that note-taking was different from liveblogging, where members of the public need to get the court's consent in advance.

The QBD's ruling does not give the press any more rights than members of the public.

But it will be welcomed by journalists, especially when they have to sit in the public gallery because the press benches are full.

The ruling only applies to taking notes and not to any kind of recording (video or audio).

CHAPTER 4

WEBSITE DISCLAIMERS, TERMS AND CONDITIONS

Media organisations should protect themselves and their online visitors by using disclaimers, and terms and conditions (T&Cs) on their websites.

A media website that allows comments and UGC should provide T&Cs that:

- Inform visitors that their anonymity cannot be guaranteed and that their details may be divulged to the courts if they post anything illegal.

- Require visitors to register their names and contact details and accept the T&Cs by proactively ticking a box, before contributing to the site.

- Explain that offensive posts may be removed if someone complains.

- Provide a robust complaints policy and 'report abuse' procedure.

- Explain users' rights under the GDPR.

Complaints Procedures

Media websites should provide a complaints procedure, a 'report abuse' button, and an email address or a form for users to use to make complaints.

If they plan to use the DA 2013's section 5 defence, they may need to institute two complaints procedures: one for defamatory comments and one for everything else, as the DA has unique procedures that might need to be dealt with separately.

Website operators should train someone to monitor complaints every day, and organise holiday, sickness and maternity cover to ensure continuity. An unacknowledged complaint could prove to be costly.

Disclaimers

Online publishers are naive if they believe that publishing an all-embracing disclaimer can exonerate them from legal risks.

Anyone who communicates anything electronically may be held liable for breaching a number of laws.

This particularly affects both freelancers and news agencies that syndicate copy and images to a broad range of organisations.

Thus, freelancers and news agencies should use a disclaimer something like this:

> 'While every effort is taken to ensure this copy is accurate and up to date, I, [Name], am not liable for any errors or inaccuracies in it.
>
> Images are subject to the copyright conditions stated at the top of the copy or embedded in the image metadata and are distributed in good faith on the basis that the copyright information is correct.

Media organisations that use copy or images provided by me accept that the decision to publish them is solely theirs and that they are responsible for all legal and ethical outcomes arising from that decision.

They should check that the copy and images conform to all relevant laws and regulatory codes, prior to publication or broadcast.

I will not accept liability for any expense, damage or loss that publishers may incur because of their decision to publish.'

Getting Online Content Removed

People who believe that an item of online content is, for example, damaging their career prospects or causing them embarrassment, may ask web editors to remove it.

There is no obligation to comply with these requests, and web editors should treat each one on its merits, and also be aware that the new DPA may apply as mentioned below (*see Chapter 5*).

Some requests to news organisations can be quite informal and easy to remedy such as the removal of the details of a person who has been featured on a dating site.

They may have met a new partner since being featured and simply want to move on.

Other take-down requests such as those from a solicitor, the police, or a government agency, should be treated more seriously.

THE RIGHT TO BE FORGOTTEN

Case Study

In May 2014, the ECJ ruled, in the case of Google Spain SL v Agencia Española de Protección de Datos, that EU citizens can request search engines to remove links to webpages that contain content that is inadequate, irrelevant, or excessive.

(5RB, n.d., *Google Spain SL v Agencia Española de Protección de Datos.*)

Google has published criteria for deciding these 'right to be forgotten' requests. They can be viewed here:

https://support.google.com/legal/answer/3110420?rd=2

The Google Spain decision does not apply to online media archives and such requests should be rebutted, as they only apply to search engine links.

However, this has not stopped people from submitting take-down requests to national and local newspapers and other online publishers.

The ICO has confirmed that media organisations might wish to consider such requests as good practice, but web editors can legitimately refuse them, using the exemption provided for journalists under the DPA.

The ruling has made it harder for journalists to research stories, as some information may have been deleted.

However, delisted content can sometimes be found via the Google cache facility. This can be accessed by searching for a website by name and selecting 'cached', by clicking on the down arrow next to the website's address in the search results.

Delisted content can also be found by searching on Google.com, which targets searchers in America. America's constitutional right to free speech gives Google the 'right to remember'.

In its transparency report in 2018, Google says it received 2.4m take-down requests between 2014 and 2017, with 43% of links being delisted as a result.

Only 8% of these were connected to crime and 7% to 'professional wrongdoing', which tends to disprove the myth that most take-down requests come from criminals trying to conceal their dubious pasts.

(Smith, 2018, *Updating Our 'Right to be Forgotten' Transparency Report.*)

In an opinion expressed in January 2019, the ECJ's Advocate General said that the right to be forgotten applied only in Europe and not worldwide. His opinion was not binding, but it is likely to be accepted when judges reac h their final verdict later this year.

(Court of Justice of the European Union, 2109, *Advocate General's Opinion in Case C-507/17, Google v CNIL.*)

Case Study

A landmark case in 2019 resulted in a dental surgeon from Amsterdam winning a ruling against Google under the right to be forgotten ruling.

The surgeon had been placed on an unofficial 'blacklist', following her suspension by a professional body because of alleged inadequate post-operative care of a patient.

She won an appeal against her suspension and then applied to have Google links to her name on the blacklist removed from search results.

It is understood that around 15 more Dutch surgeons with minor disciplinary actions against them have made similar applications. More than half have been successful.

(Lexology, 2019, *Do Professionals Have the 'Right to be Forgotten'?*)

Case Study

In the first right to be forgotten case in the UK, heard at the High Court in London, two businessman – named only as NT1 and NT2 – sought to force Google to remove details of their criminal convictions from its search results.

NT1 had been jailed in the 1990s for conspiracy to false accounting, while NT2 had been jailed for improper business dealings.

The first man's request was denied, while the second businessman won his case, with the judge stating that NT1 had shown "no remorse" and that it was in the public interest for links to remain visible.

(Inforrm, 2018, *NT1 and NT2 v Google Inc: How to Seek the Delisting of Search Engine Results Following the First English Decision on the 'Right to be Forgotten'.*)

The Surrey Comet and other newspapers have undermined ECJ rulings by running stories detailing an individual's 'right to be forgotten' request to Google.

This tactic brings the story back into the public eye and also produces a new Google hyperlink.

Case Study

In September 2015, Google was served a 'take-down' order by the ICO over links to stories held in some online media archives.

It was the first public enforcement notice served by the ICO since the 'right to be forgotten' was introduced by the ECJ in 2014.

It is likely to affect links to content in media archives and the 'public's right to know'.

The case involved an individual in the UK, who asked Google to remove a link to a story in a newspaper's archive about their conviction for a minor offence 10 years earlier.

Google complied, but the newspaper then published a story about the removal, including details of the original conviction, which was spent under the Rehabilitation of Offenders Act (ROA). Other media also published articles about it.

The individual then asked Google to remove the links to the new newspaper story, but it refused, saying they were relevant and published in the public interest. The individual then appealed to the ICO.

The ICO ruled against Google. According to David Smith, the ICO Deputy Commissioner, the individual was not involved in public life and the fact that the story breached their privacy was likely to cause them distress.

He also noted that the original conviction was not current.

Smith added that the ICO accepted that the search results related to journalistic content and were both newsworthy and in the public interest.

However, he said that the public interest could be served without doing a search using the complainant's name.

Google was given 35 days to remove the offending links or risk further enforcement action.

It considered appealing but eventually complied by changing the way it delists search results. The ICO told Online and Social Media Law that Google's new approach appeared to address its concerns.

(Wired Gov, 2015, *ICO Orders Removal of Google Search Results.*)

(ICO, 2015, *Google Inc.*)

ONLINE ABUSE

The law has been slow to respond to online abuse, and some people have behaved online in ways that would have resulted in arrest and punishment in the real world.

However, prosecutions are becoming more common.

In 2013, former director of public prosecutions Keir Starmer published guidelines for prosecutions involving online abuse and warned that people will be prosecuted if they post messages that:

- Make credible threats of violence.
- Are targeted campaigns of harassment against an individual.
- Breach court orders.
- Are grossly offensive, indecent, obscene or false.

However, the guidelines say that the authorities should take a relaxed approach to banter, humour and offensive messages, including:

- Satire and jokes that are silly or made in bad taste.

- Rudeness.

- Unpopular or unfashionable opinions.

- Distasteful and hurtful comments.

Under-18s and tweeters with few followers are less likely to be prosecuted.

Social media online abuse guidelines, which were updated in 2018, are available here:

> *http://www.cps.gov.uk/legal/a_to_c/communications_sent_via_social_media/*

The government published a white paper in 2019 aimed at curbing online abuse, and which proposed that social media platforms have a statutory "duty of care" towards users.

The Online Harms White Paper proposes a new regulatory framework to protect people online from "illegal and unacceptable content".

There is particular emphasis in the white paper on the protection of children from online bullying and abuse and on curbing the spread of terrorist propaganda or fake news with the potential to undermine democracy.

A new online regulator is proposed to oversee whether companies are limiting the spread of online harm and exercising their duty of care.

(Mayhew, 2019, *Online Harms White Paper*.)

Exposing Abusers

Online abuse victims can apply to the High Court for a 'Norwich Pharmacal' injunction to force a webmaster to provide details of posters' internet service provider addresses or names.

However, social media websites like Facebook and Twitter are based in the US and are not subject to UK / EU laws.

During 2018, Facebook received 15,262 requests for user data from the UK, affecting 19,896 users.

(Facebook, 2018, *Government Requests for User Data.*)

Other figures show that Twitter responded to 947 account information requests in the first six months of 2018, with information being released in 70% of these cases.

(Twitter, 2018, *Transparency Report: Information Requests.*)

Twitter allows users to report abusive tweets, profiles or messages. Its 'mute' button was extended in April 2019 to prevent tweets containing chosen keywords or phrases from appearing in the notifications bar.

The mute function allows users to remove tweets from their timelines without having to unfollow or block accounts.

Users can also opt out of seeing conversations that include these keywords. Users can also use the mute button to exclude tweets from individual accounts.

There are also additional categories of offensive material. People who wish to object to a tweet can do so here:

https://help.twitter.com/en/safety-and-security/report-abusive-behavior

They can also contact Lumen at *https://lumendatabase.org/* which will evaluate the complaint according to US law and publish its findings on its website.

Content writers and journalists who experience abuse should store copies of any relevant offensive material, including screenshots, for use in any subsequent court proceedings.

In 2014, internet troll David Limond was jailed for six months for abusive online messages sent to magazine journalist Angela Haggerty.

(HoldtheFrontPage, 2014, *Internet Troll Jailed for Abusing Journalist.*)

Express and Star journalist Annabal Bagdi received online abuse following an article she wrote about the benefits of immigration.

Annabal told HoldtheFrontPage: "I always knew there would be a mixed reaction to my column on immigration, but I didn't expect some of the abusive comments and personal attacks which came along with it."

(HoldtheFrontPage, 2018, *Journalist Hits Back at Trolls after Immigration Column Sparked Personal Abuse.*)

Case Study

A self-confessed white supremacist and anti-Semite was jailed for a year in 2018 after posting racist messages on her blog, which praised Hitler as a "good man".

Barbara Fielding-Morriss, 79, who stood as an independent candidate during local elections in Stoke-on-Trent in 2017, was convicted of three counts of stirring up racial hatred.

She posted that she wanted Britain to be "white only" and that the country faced "annihilation" from immigrants.

(BBC News, 2018, *Stoke-on-Trent Central Candidate Jailed for Race Hate Crimes*.)

Case Study

A UKIP candidate in the 2019 European elections, Carl Benjamin, refused to apologise after sending a tweet to MP Jess Phillips, which said: "I wouldn't even rape you."

The Labour MP for Birmingham Yardley said that as a result of the tweet she received 600 threats of rape.

Benjamin refused to apologise for the tweet to the MP and claimed he was being targeted by the media for "crimes against political correctness" (Walker, 2019, *YouTuber Accused of Triggering Rape Threats Could Stand for UKIP*).

For media companies and website operators, a moral decision may sometimes have to be taken to disable user comments 'below the line', if they become abusive. However, this can compromise the libel defences of 'no moderation'.

Aside from the normal considerations of moderation and legal responsibility, some content provokes a diatribe of abuse from people visiting particular websites.

Both the Bradford Argus and the Bolton News have suspended comments because of online abuse.

In the latter, it was because of racist abuse in response to a particular story; in the former, a decision was taken to suspend comments on all stories for a length of time.

Laws That Can be Used Against Abusers

Trolling, cyberbullying and abuse fall into the following categories, as far as the law is concerned.

Death Threats

Perpetrators may be prosecuted under the Offences Against the Person Act 1861.

Stalking

Communications that target specific individuals may be treated as stalking, under the Protection from Harassment Act (PHA) 1997.

There have been no prosecutions to date because cyberbullies and abusers hide behind anonymity, and prosecutions must be brought against named individuals.

Harassment

Under the PHA, someone who sends two or more messages to the same person can be prosecuted and served with an injunction, if they cause that person alarm or distress.

Malicious Falsehood

A person can be sued if they publish false statements that are intended to damage a person or their business, commercial interests, goods or services.

Gross Offence, Indecency, Obscenity or Menace

The Communications Act (CA) 2003 applies to posts that are grossly offensive and could cause fear or apprehension.

The latest Crime Survey for England and Wales showed that computer misuse offences fell from 1,227 in the year ending March 2018, to 966 during the same period the following year.

(Office for National Statistics, 2019, *Crime in England and Wales: year ending March 2019.*)

Case Study

In 2018, 30-year-old Mark Meechan was convicted of a hate crime by a court in Lanarkshire, after posting a video of his girlfriend's dog giving a Nazi salute.

He was prosecuted under the CA after the video – in which the dog can be seen responding to phrases such as 'Sieg Heil' – was viewed more than 3m times on YouTube.

He was fined £800 for making what the judge said was grossly offensive material, which was anti-Semitic in nature.

(Dearden, 2018, *Man Who Taught Girlfriend's Pet Pug to Perform Nazi Salutes Fined £800.*)

Fraud

Anyone who impersonates someone using a false social media account can be prosecuted under the Fraud Act (FA) 2006, if the account gives a misleading or untrue impression and causes the person loss or damage.

Pranksters often misuse Twitter by impersonating celebrities, famous people and businesses. Twitter provides an online complaints form for victims. Blatant misrepresentation may also lead to prosecution for identity theft.

Journalists and bloggers should check the validity of social media accounts before quoting from them.

Threatening Behaviour

Messages may be illegal if they make someone believe that physical harm is imminent, or if they threaten someone with violence or damage to their property.

Promoting Terrorism

The Terrorism Act 2006 makes it an offence to publish statements that directly or indirectly encourage people to commit, prepare, or instigate acts of terrorism.

Case Study

In 2018, an engineer from Newcastle was jailed for seven years for sharing videos on Facebook that included terrorism-related material.

Abdulrahman Alcharbati was also convicted of being in possession of a bomb-making manual.

The court heard that Alcharbati had made 70 posts that glorified terrorism, with one video showing Syrian soldiers being beaten to death.

(BBC News, 2018, *Abdulrahman Alcharbati Jailed for Terrorism Facebook Videos*.)

Revealing Personal Information

Trolls and online abusers often use people's personal information. But this should not be published without the consent of the individual involved, unless it is already in the public domain, or publication is in the public interest.

Personal privacy is protected by the:

- DPA 2018.

- ECHR Article 8 (privacy).

- Ipso / Ofcom codes of practice.

These cover personal information such as:

- Medical details.

- Financial information.

- Work records.

- Family relationships.

- Sexual conduct.

- Emotional / mental state.

- Written or digital correspondence.

- Social media records such as information or photos from private Facebook or social media accounts.

In 2017, the ICO launched an investigation into the way in which social media companies and other organisations use personal data, especially for political purposes. Facebook was one of 30 organisations investigated.

It followed the Cambridge Analytica scandal, in which the personal data of more than 1 million UK citizens on Facebook was shared with the political consultancy firm.

The data was collected from a third-party app called 'thisisyourdigitallife'.

It recommended that users of social media should review their privacy settings, particularly following updates, and produced a series of factsheets relating to various social media such as Twitter, Facebook and Instagram.

It also produced advice regarding microtargeting, a form of online targeted advertising.

(ICO, 2018, Social Media Privacy Settings.)

The ICO's investigation was concluded in November 2018 and the ICO has submitted a report to parliament.

This can be read here: *https://ico.org.uk/media/action-weve-taken/2260271/investigation-into-the-use-of-data-analytics-in-political-campaigns-final-20181105.pdf*

Photos usually represent a more significant invasion of privacy than words.

Under-16s have greater privacy rights. This was established in the case of Weller and Others v Associated Newspapers Limited, as noted in the case study below.

Case Study

In 2012, the Mail Online published unpixelated photos of singer Paul Weller's three children aged 10 months to 16 years.

The singer sued for a breach of privacy and won £10,000 in damages, despite the Mail Online arguing that the photos were innocuous and taken in a public place.

In March 2016, the Supreme Court refused Associated Newspapers' permission to appeal against a ruling by the Court of Appeal, which said that although children do not have separate privacy rights, they may have a reasonable expectation of privacy on occasions where an adult does not.

Publishers should take into account factors such as:

- The child's attributes.
- What they are doing, and where.
- The nature and purpose of the intrusion.
- Whether consent was given.
- The effect on the child.

The ruling effectively prevents the media from publishing images of children without consent.

(Courts and Tribunals Judiciary, 2012, *Weller v Associated Newspapers Ltd.*)

Case Study

Ipso rejected a complaint in 2017 from a mother who said that a picture of her 13-year-old son featured on the front page of Portsmouth News, alongside football "hooligans" wanted by police, was a breach of the Editors' Code of Practice (clause 6, children).

The mother said she had not consented to the picture being used and that its publication had caused the family distress.

For its part, the paper said that the image had come from the police and that because it showed a pitch invasion by fans, there was a public interest defence in it being published.

Ipso said there was "exceptional public interest" in the picture being used because it exposed potential criminal activity.

(Ipso, 2017, 19498-17 *Perrin v The News (Portsmouth).*)

Case Study

In March 2016, the Court of Appeal issued an interim injunction preventing the Sun on Sunday from revealing the identity of a married celebrity who had been involved in a sexual threesome.

The injunction remains in place and means that no UK media can name the man, even though he has been named in other countries, and on social media.

The case was referred to the Supreme Court, which ruled, in May 2016, that the injunction should remain in force.

(BAILII, EWCA Civ 100, 2016.)

Hate Crimes

In the online environment, the criminal offences mentioned in the section _Online Abuse_ above can also be defined as hate crimes, if they constitute hostility or prejudice based on:

- Disability.
- Race.
- Religion.
- Transgender identity.
- Sexual orientation.

If there is evidence of a hate crime when someone is convicted for another offence, the judge can impose a tougher sentence under the CJA 2003.

Hate crime law has raised concerns from some writers and journalists about freedom of speech.

'Hatred' is subjective, and some critics have attached the 'hate' label to comments that are simply robust debates, criticism or satire.

Case Study

The leader and deputy leader of the far-right organisation Britain First were jailed in 2018 for hate crimes after they posted online videos of themselves racially abusing innocent people.

Paul Golding and Jayda Fransen were each convicted, at Folkestone Magistrates Court, of a series of hate crimes, after targeting people they thought were connected to a gang-rape trial.

The pair had filmed themselves banging on the window of a takeaway shop shouting "paedophile" and "foreigner".

The videos were posted online but the court heard that the shop owners were not connected with the trial.

Judge Justin Barron said the pair took part in "a campaign to draw attention to the race, religion and immigrant background of the defendants" (BBC News, 2018, *Britain First Leader and Deputy Leader Jailed for Hate Crimes*).

Sexting

The Criminal Justice and Courts Act 2015 makes sexting or 'revenge porn', a crime.

Anyone who sends or receives a sexually explicit text, image or video footage on a mobile phone or tablet, or posts them online, with intent to cause distress, can be charged.

This law may cause an ethical dilemma for editors, as it does not provide complainants with anonymity if they are over 18.

This lack of protection may deter victims from making a complaint to the police, and media coverage could draw further attention to the offensive images and make a complaint counter-productive.

However, if complainants were given anonymity, then it would be likely that the identities of their alleged abusers may also be protected, as naming them would reveal the names of the complainants.

As things stand, the only option for complainants is to apply for witness anonymity under the Coroners and Justice Act 2009 or to ask their solicitor to apply for a section 11 order under the CoCA 1981, if the allegation resulted in a court case.

However, web editors must be prepared for victims to ask them to provide anonymity voluntarily. There is certainly an ethical argument for doing so.

Journalists investigating allegations of sexting should strongly discourage alleged victims from sending them the images involved.

They may inadvertently commit an offence under the Protection of Children Act (PCA) 1978, by storing indecent images of a person under 18 on a smartphone or other device. This can make investigating allegations of paedophilia unsafe.

Online Security and Privacy

Protecting Sources

In 2013, former Guardian newspaper editor Alan Rusbridger made an important speech reminding everybody that journalists had a duty to protect their sources.

This convention does not apply to content writers and bloggers.

The Ipso and Ofcom codes require journalists to protect confidential sources of information.

In addition, the CoCA says journalists should only reveal sources if a High Court judge passes an order for them to do so in the interests of justice or national security, or for the prevention of disorder or crime.

A judge must consider freedom of expression under the ECHR when considering passing an order.

Journalists should reveal the source of a story only to their editor or line manager, and they should take professional and legal advice if a police officer or government official asks them to reveal a source.

Case Study

In August 2015, the Big Issue North published an interview with a victim of a Rotherham sex abuse gang.

The interview had been commissioned by a freelance journalist. (Big Issue North, 2015, *They Don't Scare Me Now*.)

A few months later, a National Crime Agency investigator emailed the editor, Kevin Gopal, asking for a meeting so that the police could recover anything held by Big Issue North relating to the published article or otherwise, to assist them with the investigation.

Mr Gopal declined. He told the investigator that he had a duty to protect his sources and was not legally obliged to hand over journalistic material.

He also advised the freelance journalist to secure the material, in case the police tried to use the Regulation of Investigatory Powers Act (Ripa) to obtain it.

In a blog post in 2017, Ipso's director of operations Charlotte Dewer revealed that the regulator had not upheld a single complaint under clause 14 of the Editors' Code of Practice, which states that journalists have a moral obligation to protect their sources.

However, she went on to state that digital media is making it increasingly difficult for journalists to protect sources.

She said: "I don't think we will see a day soon when Ipso's complaints committee will uphold a breach of the code on the basis that a journalist communicated with a source via Dropbox rather than Snapchat, or the other way round.

"But Ipso will continue to be aware of the context in which it operates when considering any concerns that confidential sources have not received the protection they are due and need in order to make disclosures that benefit all of us as members of the public."

She cited a report titled Journalists' Sources, Surveillance and Whistleblowing, by the Institute of Advanced Legal Studies (IALS), which lays out the issues in a clear-sighted way.

(IALS, 2017, *Journalists' Sources, Surveillance and Whistleblowing*.)

The same report by the IALS recommends increased training for journalists and the media in how to protect sources in the digital age, including "legal, technological and psychological" factors.

It warns that there may be limits to such protection and that potential sources should be made aware of this.

(IALS, 2017, *Protecting Sources and Whistleblowers in a Digital Age*.)

In practice, social media and Instant Messages (IM) make it difficult for journalists to keep their contacts secure.

To avoid unintentionally exposing sources, they should:

- Provide a secure online shared folder for sensitive documents.

- Tell sources not to communicate with them via email or public social media pages.

- Check to whom they are connected on LinkedIn and similar websites. Their contacts might not want other people to know that they are connected to a journalist or blogger.

- Beware of tweeting that they are meeting someone, and remember to turn off location services when meeting contacts privately.

- Use separate social media accounts for work, and choose 'friends' carefully.

- Use messaging apps like WhatsApp that provide encryption.

Risks Posed by the 'Grim Ripa' and its Successor

The Regulation of Investigatory Powers Act 2000 (Ripa) was replaced by the Investigatory Powers Act 2016 (IPA).

Ripa proved to be one of the most controversial pieces of legislation to have affected journalists, and the IPA may present an even graver threat.

Ripa gave the police and some other public authorities the power to apply to the home secretary for an order that allowed them to access a journalist's email messages, phone records and other digital data.

For example, police investigating the former MP Chris Huhne's speeding fraud secretly obtained a Mail on Sunday reporter's phone records without his consent.

(O'Carroll, 2014, Police Secretly Obtained Reporter's Phone Records in Huhne Investigation.)

In another incident, police investigating the 'Plebgate' saga obtained the phone records of the Sun newspaper's political editor, Tom Newton Dunn.

(O'Carroll, 2014, *Plebgate: Met Obtained Phone Records of Sun Political Editor without Consent*.)

These examples were the tip of the iceberg. Figures showed that the police made more than 6,000 Ripa applications in 2013 compared with just over 60 in 2002.

The IPA became law in December 2016. It requires web and phone companies to store records of websites visited by every citizen (including journalists) for 12 months, for access by police, security services and other public bodies.

It also allows security services to acquire bulk collections of communications data such as mobile phone records.

The Act gives special protection to journalists' data and sources, but many critics fear these measures do not go far enough and have labelled it the 'Snoopers' Charter'.

The Office of Surveillance Commissioners was replaced by the Investigatory Powers Commissioner's Office, in 2017.

Case Study

In 2019, campaign group Liberty lost a High Court challenge to the use of IPA.

Liberty had sought a judicial review of the law, arguing that its mass surveillance powers were in breach of human rights, but judges argued that the legislation contained safeguards against such abuses.

(Goodwin, 2018, *Liberty Heads for Judicial Review over Investigatory Powers Act.*)

(Courts and Tribunals Judiciary, 2019, *Liberty Judgment Final*.)

Safe Digital Practice

Unfortunately, many editorial computer systems do not allow reporters to browse anonymously and do not offer basic encryption, and the webmasters can easily read email messages sent to and from journalists' work email accounts.

When working on sensitive stories, journalists should:

- Use a private, encrypted browser like Tor. If their office computers do not allow this, they should browse on another device.

- Use a personal, encrypted webmail account for sensitive stories.

- Encrypt IMs and scramble social media conversations, when possible.

- Secure their home wifi networks.

- Use complex passwords on all web accounts.

- Make phone calls using a pay-as-you-go mobile phone, paid for in cash or with an Amazon voucher or similar.

- Record contacts' details in a paper book, and store it securely at home.

- Avoid promising someone anonymity, unless they are certain they can achieve it.

Journalists should bear in mind that if contacts are stored on an employer's computer, those contacts belong to the employer, and they could be in breach of the DPA and GDPR if they download the contacts when leaving the company.

GDPR rules state that the processing of data is the responsibility of organisations.

Procedures should be in place to prevent disgruntled employees, or merely those leaving a company, from taking personal data with them.

The same applies to their contacts on LinkedIn and similar platforms.

If staff members use their employers' computer facilities and their business email address to create a LinkedIn account, courts are likely to consider the content as belonging to the employer.

Since journalists and bloggers are often recruited because of the quality and breadth of their contacts, they are advised to keep copies of their own contacts at home.

Computer Misuse

Everyone has a legal and ethical duty to respect other people's digital privacy.

The infamous phone hacking trial showed beyond doubt that it is a criminal offence under the Computer Misuse Act (CMA) to hack someone's phone, mobile phone, tablet or computer, or to alter, transfer or copy files without permission.

In addition, clause 10 of the Editors' Code of Practice states: "The press must not seek to obtain or publish material acquired by using hidden cameras or clandestine listening devices; or by intercepting private or mobile phone calls, messages or emails; or by the unauthorised removal of documents or photos; or by accessing digitally-held private information without consent" (Ipso, 2019, *Editors' Code of Practice*).

This clause can be breached in the public interest, but no such defence exists under the CMA.

Archiving Digital Data and Images

Website operators, journalists and bloggers should retain digital data in case they receive a complaint or need to use the data to deal with a complaint, or in a court case.

Courts also have the power to request disclosure of deleted documents and can impose penalties on anyone attempting to amend or delete documents that might be required as evidence.

Staff journalists and content writers who use their own digital devices or social media accounts for work can cause problems.

This is because their editors or publishers might not be able to access the data, should it be required.

However, if they do use their own devices and accounts, they should comply with their employers' Bring Your Own Device Policy and Safeguarding Information on Mobile Devices Policy under the GDPR.

Web editors and webmasters should set clear rules about data retention for IM, email, web activity logs, text messages, and history from Facebook, Twitter and similar channels.

Online Archives

Online archives can present a range of legal problems. Listed below are the main risks related to them.

Defamation

Online publishers who republish defamatory items may be liable for libel, but have some protection under the DA 2013.

See the section called '_What a libel claimant must prove_', under Defamation, above.

Case Study

In February 2014, the High Court ruled that an archived news report could lose the protection of qualified privilege, should circumstances change.

The ruling, in the case of Flood v Times Newspapers Limited, means that publishers should consider updating or amending online content if someone who once faced an accusation has since been cleared.

(5RB, n.d., _Flood v Times Newspapers Limited_.)

QCs Hugh Tomlinson and Guy Vassall-Adams of Matrix Chambers have written about such dangers in their book Online Publications Claims: A Guide (2017).

They state: "A link that appears on the first page of a Google search against a person's name is a constant point of reference for all those who meet or deal with that person.

"This means that, in contrast to traditional media publications, it is not safe simply to ignore false or private material published online" (Matrix Chambers, 2017, *Matrix Launches 'Online Publication Claims: A Practical Guide'*).

In addition, Ofcom or Ipso may order webmasters running UK magazine and newspaper websites to remove items that have breached the respective codes of practice.

Restricted Identities

An online archive may contain content or images of someone who subsequently receives legal anonymity.

It is safe to retain the content, but attention should not be drawn to it, nor should articles include new links to it, either manually or automatically.

'Similar stories' tools can cause problems here and need to be monitored.

Web editors should respond quickly to legitimate take-down requests from courts, the police or the AG.

Use of Incorrect Images

Using an incorrect photo from an archive can be defamatory, especially if used to depict a criminal or someone involved in insalubrious activities.

Archived photos should be tagged with clear identification details, especially if the photos include images of people who have common names.

Case Study

In November 2013, E! Online published a picture of Steps's singer Ian 'H' Watkins instead of the Lostprophets's frontman, Ian Watkins, when reporting a child abuse case.

Paedophile Ian Watkins, 36, of Pontypridd, lead singer of the now-disbanded rock group Lostprophets, admitted, at Cardiff Crown Court, to a string of child sex abuse charges, including the attempted rape of a baby.

In a statement, an E! Online spokeswoman said: "E! Online deeply regrets originally publishing an image of Ian 'H' Watkins of the band Steps, rather than Ian Watkins of Lostprophets, and the error was corrected immediately" (Carter, 2013, *Steps Star H Wins Public Apology after Being Wrongly Pictured as Paedophile*).

Stock Images

Reusing archived photos may breach an individual's right to privacy. A web editor or blogger may need fresh consent to use a photo in a story with a different context.

For example, a news website might publish (with consent) a photo of a man smoking outside a hospital's accident and emergency department while waiting to see if his wife had survived a serious car accident.

But it would probably be a breach of the man's privacy rights if the website later used the same image to accompany a feature on the effects of smoking in later life.

Just because someone consents to being photographed in one situation does not mean they have given their consent to reuses in other circumstances.

In addition, it is wise to check copyright arrangements on stock images or free ones, in case they change over time.

Some copyright owners of images that may have originally been free to use under a CCL may now demand a fee for usage. Moral rights also apply here.

Other Dangers

Other dangers are as follows:

- Republishing an article about a defendant's conviction may be defamatory, if they have since been cleared on appeal.

- Republishing old court copy means that the libel protection drops from absolute privilege to qualified privilege, which stipulates that copy should not be published with malice.

- Republishing details of someone's previous crimes and convictions could breach the ROA 1974. Again, publishing with malice could create a problem defending a libel claim.

- As mentioned above, a website's automatic 'similar stories' function might display someone's previous convictions or other information, which could prejudice another trial.

- An article or photo may refer to changed circumstances.

  For instance, a story about a husband and wife who were happily married could be defamatory if republished when they had since separated and married other people.

Another example might be where a person has changed gender and there are libel issues regarding publication.

Case Study

As well as the dangers of libel, there is the risk of accidentally emailing confidential material to the wrong person.

In 2019, the High Court granted an injunction after an officer for the Advertising Standards Authority (ASA) inadvertently sent an email containing confidential information to someone involved in a dispute with the authority.

The interim injunction was granted after a 'recall' email was ignored by Robert Mitchell, the subject of a complaint to the ASA.

The recall email requested that the original email be deleted and that none of the confidential contents be published or communicated to others.

Mr Justice Warby said it would have been obvious to Mr Mitchell that the contents were confidential and that there was no public interest defence in the contents being made public.

(BAILII, 2019, EWHC 1469.)

Chapter 5

Data Protection

The Data Protection Act 1998 was replaced by the Data Protection Act (DPA) 2018 and sets out the framework for data protection law in the UK.

The new law sits alongside the EU's General Data Protection Regulation (GDPR) and tailors how the GDPR applies in the UK.

It provides exemptions for journalists and people who write online for artistic and literary purposes.

A range of restrictions apply to media organisations that store people's names, addresses and other personal information securely and they have a duty to process it fairly and lawfully.

The Act gives people the right to ask media organisations for a copy of information held about them, using a 'subject access request'.

However, editors can reject these requests and avoid most other requirements under the DPA by using the journalistic exemption. If they do so, the person who requested the information can complain to the ICO, Ipso or Ofcom.

Although such complaints are unlikely to succeed, media organisations must have procedures for handling subject access requests, especially as the 'right to be forgotten' ruling, mentioned earlier, may trigger more requests.

ICO guidance for the media states that in using the exemption, publishers must weigh up whether publishing the data would be in the public interest, taking into account the BBC Editorial Guidelines, the Ofcom Broadcasting Code, and the Editors' Code of Practice.

It said on its website: "We expect you to be able to explain why the exemption is required in each case, and how and by whom this was considered at the time. The ICO does not have to agree with your view – but we must be satisfied that you had a reasonable belief" (ICO, n.d., *Exemptions*).

For the media and journalists, as well as for others who process data for academic, literary or artistic purposes, the exemptions are known as 'special purposes'.

These originally featured under section 32 of the DPA 1998 and have been expanded as part of Schedule 2 of the 2018 Act.

The beefed-up special exemption protection provided for the media under Schedule 2, part 5, of the DPA 2018 means that journalists no longer have to prove that processing of data is for journalistic special purposes only, as was previously the case.

In other words, if the data was used for other, secondary purposes, then the defence can still be used.

The special purposes exemptions contained within the Act can be found here:

http://www.legislation.gov.uk/ukpga/2018/12/part/6/crossheading/the-special-purposes/enacted

As stated above, the law makes it clear that journalists and others can only call upon the special purposes defence if:

- Processing of data is carried out with a view to publication.

- Publication is in the public interest.

- They believe that compliance with the Act would be at odds with special purposes.

The ICO also makes it clear that the exemption cannot be relied on as a blanket defence, as has been the assumption in the past.

(ICO, 2018, *Data Protection and Journalism: How to Complain about Media Organisations* .)

The ICO has also said: "You should not routinely rely on exemptions; you should consider them on a case-by-case basis. They do not need to respond to requests about the data they hold, or removal requests" (ICO, 2018, *Guide to the General Data Protection Regulation* (GDPR)).

On the flipside, PRs sending press releases to journalists need to get explicit consent from recipients.

This places them in a potentially difficult position if the content is construed as marketing, as opposed to information, and if the request is also viewed as an unsolicited email.

In 2019, Google in France was ordered to pay a €50m fine under the new GDPR for failing to gain consent for processing data.

(Lexology, 2019, *Google Ordered to Pay First Multi-Million GDPR Fine.*)

And on a more prosaic level, in another case, a church worker in Sweden was fined €400 for including the personal details of parishioners without their consent on a church website she created as a parish magazine.

Case Study

Morrisons was held "vicariously liable" when an employee leaked personal details – including bank details – of more than 90,000 employees onto the internet in a mass data breach and lost its case at the Court of Appeal.

It has now been granted leave to appeal against the decision to the Supreme Court. The case has been set for November 2019.

The supermarket argues that it is not liable because the breach was made by an employee who had a grudge against the company.

(Inforrm, 2019, *News: Supreme Court Grants Permission To Appeal In The Morrisons Mass Data Breach Case.*)

Case Study

Online pregnancy club Bounty, which distributes free packs to pregnant women in hospital, was fined £400,000 in 2019 for a breach of section 55a of the DPA 1998, after it was found to have shared the personal data of 14 million new mums to 39 different companies.

No consent had been given for the sharing of personal data, which was given in good faith when the pregnancy packs were given out, and the ICO found it had processed the data unfairly by acting as a data broker.

(ICO, 2019, *Bounty UK Fined £400,000 for Sharing Personal Data Unlawfully.*)

Case Study

In 2018, at the High Court, a UK expert in the medical dangers of asbestos, Dr Robin Rudd, successfully applied for a subject access request against the firm of John Bridle. Bridle disputed what Rudd claimed were links between asbestos and health problems.

Rudd had requested that Bridle desist from processing his personal data. The court ruled that Bridle could not rely on any of the three defences for failure to comply with a subject access request.

(BAILLI, 2019, EWHC 893.)

Journalists and Data Protection Offences

The DPA makes it a criminal offence for a journalist to knowingly or recklessly obtain personal data from another organisation without its consent; for example, by subterfuge, misrepresentation or hacking.

The offence provides a public interest defence, but a stricter threshold is applied.

Use of Drones

Many UK media organisations and bloggers use drones to shoot video footage in difficult locations, or for news stories and investigative assignments.

Journalists are entitled to use drones for surveillance, provided they are necessary and that the story is in the public interest under the Ipso and Ofcom regulatory codes.

These activities are also covered by the DPA, although the journalistic exemption applies.

However, the ICO has advised the media to be open and honest with the public when they are using drones, as they can arouse concern.

Some media organisations use signs to tell the public when they are filming.

If someone complains about covert filming, the ICO will weigh up the:

- Importance of the story.

- Level of intrusion.

- Potential impact upon the individual and any third parties.

The Civil Aviation Authority (CAA) has a series of guidelines for drones and other unmanned aircraft.

In 2014, it issued a photographer from Lancashire with a caution for using a drone for commercial gain without permission, after the photographer sold footage of a fire at a school to media organisations.

(Civil Aviation Authority, 2015, *Unmanned Aircraft and Drones*.)

Media organisations may wish to check that this ruling does not affect their operations.

Case Study

In 2015, Ipso (House v Express.co.uk) ruled there had been no breach of privacy in a newspaper's use of a drone to take footage following a gas explosion at a property.

The drone captured images of the damaged home and the occupant complained that it "showed the contents of her home which were not visible to members of the public, including her bathroom, stairs and bedroom".

But Ipso said the footage was not intrusive and, given that the incident was both serious and newsworthy: "The complainant did not have a reasonable expectation that her property was a private place" (Ipso, 2015, 07063-15 *House v Express.co.uk*).

Cookies

The current cookie law came into force in 2011 through amendments to the Privacy and Electronic Communications (EC Directive) Regulations.

As a result, pop-up consent boxes have become common on most websites.

Cookies are small text files that are placed on a person's computer when they visit a website. They enable the website to recognise the person each time they visit it.

However, they can only be used if they are strictly necessary for:

- Communication to take place between the user and the website.

Or:

- To provide a service that the user has requested.

The user must give consent to cookies that are used for other purposes.

However, the law was amended at the end of March 2019, to ensure that 'consent' meets the higher standards required by the GDPR.

In July 2019, the ICO issued strict new guidance about consent.

The definition of 'strictly necessary' has been amended to distinguish between 'session cookies' and 'persistent cookies'.

Session cookies are used for one-off visitors, whereas persistent cookies are for people who visit the same website regularly.

There are tighter controls on cookies that are used for more than one purpose, some of which are strictly necessary and some not.

Consent is now needed for all purposes, unless they fall within the 'strictly necessary' exemption.

Consent must be informed. Websites must provide clear information about what cookies are used, and why.

If third-party cookies are used, the website must clearly and specifically name who the third parties are, and explain what they will do with the information.

Consent must be active, and cannot be pre-set as a default option.

If a user continues to use a website after being notified of the use of cookies, it does not mean they have given consent. They must tick a box, or click an 'Accept' button.

The options to consent to or refuse cookies should have equal prominence. A large 'Accept' button and small 'Reject' link will not suffice.

The user should not be able to use the site before they give consent.

This means that some websites will have to introduce an overlaid Consent page, which only disappears once the user has given consent.

Cookie walls, which block general access to a website if consent is not provided, do not constitute valid consent, as the user has no choice but to accept cookies if they want to use the site.

Users should be regularly asked to reconfirm their preferences.

The ICO has not set a deadline for compliance, but Ali Shah, head of technology policy, said in a blog in July 2019: "Start working towards compliance now – undertake a cookie audit, document your decisions, and you will have nothing to fear."

However, the post adds: "Cookie compliance will be an increasing regulatory priority for the ICO in the future" (ICO, 2019, *Blog: Cookies – what does 'good' look like?*).

LAWS ENABLING ACCESS TO INFORMATION

There are some laws that can help journalists, bloggers, etc, to gather information.

Freedom of Information Act (FOIA) 2000

This law gives anyone the right to access information held by more than 100,000 publicly funded bodies, ranging from hospitals and schools to quangos and government departments.

Since its inception in 2005, it has provided journalists, bloggers and campaigning websites with information for countless stories that would not otherwise have been reported.

These include the infamous MPs' expenses scandal of 2009 and the report in July 2015 that UK pilots had taken part in coalition airstrikes over Syria.

Revelations like these may explain why former Prime Minister Tony Blair, in his memoirs, called himself a "foolish, irresponsible nincompoop" for introducing the Act (Blair, 2011, A Journey).

The Act allows anyone, the press and the public, to make written requests for information from any public body.

The body must respond within 20 working days and may not ask why the information is being requested.

If the body concerned refuses a request, it must usually provide a reason, and it can reject vexatious requests or those that are disproportionately expensive.

(ICO, n.d., When Can We Refuse a Request for Information?)

If information appears to have been wrongly withheld, the person who asked for it can complain to the ICO.

There was some concern in 2015 when the government announced a review of the FOIA. The media feared that the Independent Commission on Freedom of Information would limit the Act's scope.

However, the review's report said there was no evidence that the FOIA needed substantial amendments.

The government accepted its recommendations in February 2016 and said the Act did not require any legal changes.

Exempt Categories

The Act lists 23 types of exemptions that bodies can use to avoid disclosing information. The exemptions can be seen here: *https://www.lboro.ac.uk/data-privacy/foi/exemptions/*

Anyone who believes that an information request has been turned down for the wrong reasons should initially complain to the body involved, and ask them to review the decision.

If this does not produce a satisfactory outcome, they can complain to the ICO, which will try to resolve the issues informally.

If they are still dissatisfied with the outcome, they can take the matter further, using the ICO's complaints process, which can be found on this downloadable pdf:

> *https://ico.org.uk/media/for-organisations/documents/1215/complaints_guide_for_public_authorities.pdf*

Case Study

In 2015, Tom Wall, an environmental journalist and digital editor of the Environmental Health News, achieved a victory over the ICO in his attempt to obtain information about bad landlords, under the FOIA.

Environmental Health News is the official magazine for the Chartered Institute of Environmental Health.

A tribunal ordered the MoJ to hand over the information on convicted landlords to Wall after it rejected the ICO's decision that the information should be kept secret.

Wall wanted details of landlords convicted of environmental health offences under the Housing Act 2004, so that local authorities could be warned about using them in the future.

The landlords had been convicted for failing to meet government standards of accommodation such as warmth and provision of basic facilities.

It took Wall more than a year to win his case, after his Freedom of Information request was rejected by the MoJ and then the ICO.

The ICO said the information was "sensitive personal data" and rejected Wall's public interest argument.

However, the First-Tier (Information Rights) Tribunal unanimously ruled in Wall's favour.

(Information Tribunal, 2015, *Appeal No: EA/2014/0265.*)

Wall told Online and Social Media Law: "It is troubling that is took me so long to obtain this information. It should have been freely available to the press.

"Many journalists would have been forced to give up long ago. I'm lucky I have generous and supportive colleagues who allowed me to pursue this story to the very end.

"But how many other good leads have been abandoned by hard-pressed reporters and campaigners without the time to challenge Britain's culture of unthinking official secrecy?"

(Thom, 2015, *Tom Wall Has Won a Freedom of Information Battle in a War that Journalists Should Not Have to Fight*).

Wall's observations confirm what many journalists feared when the FOIA was introduced.

It is a law that cuts both ways. It gives them access to some information, but it also enables authorities to withhold other material, or make it too difficult and expensive to access it.

How to Submit a Request

Requests under the FOIA must be made to the authority's information officer or equivalent.

They should be specific and state the exact nature of the information required, and if possible, the timescale. For example: 'Can I have data on the number of homeless people in Swindon from 2013-2015.'

However, many people use the excellent website *https://www.whatdotheyknow.com/* for FOIA requests.

(What DoTheyKnow, n.d., *Browse and Search Requests*.)

This website has archived almost 300,000 FOIA responses from more than 16,000 public bodies. New requests can be submitted using an online form.

Environmental Information Regulations (EIR) 2004

The EIR is similar to the FOIA but applies to information relating to the environment.

Anyone researching anything from GM crops to flooding, and climate change to swine flu can ask public authorities to provide them with information. EIR requests can be made verbally.

However, as with the FOIA, the EIR has exemptions that allow the body to reject information requests by sending the requester a refusal notice.

The exemptions include unfinished documents, internal communications, requests that are "manifestly unreasonable", or those where disclosure would be harmful.

The EIR is administered by the ICO, which has a separate complaints procedure that can be used. See details:

https://ico.org.uk/for-organisations/guide-to-the-environmental-information-regulations/complaints/

Data Protection Act (DPA) 2018

Journalists tend to see the DPA as an enemy but, in fact, they can use it to research stories by asking a contact to access their personal information from an authority and pass it to the journalist to use in a story.

These rights existed in the DPA 1998 but have been transferred to the DPA 2018.

For instance, a journalist doing a story about a mistake made in a hospital operation could get general information about the operation using the FOIA, if necessary.

And they could ask the person they are writing about to request their personal medical files from the hospital, under the DPA.

Although the DPA invariably trumps FOIA requests that involve personal information, journalists can argue that information should be released in the public interest, if it concerns an official's public role.

For instance, a journalist may be investigating a story about the chair of a quango who has allegedly used his influence to give a top job to an unqualified friend.

The friend's details would normally be protected by the DPA. However, the journalist might be able to access her CV under the FOIA, arguing that her private information has a significant impact on her public role.

Case Studies

Two rulings by the First-tier Tribunal (Information Rights) in early 2016 demonstrate the balancing act that authorities must perform when considering FOIA requests that involve people's personal details.

The tribunal ruled that Swansea Council was not required to release details of an internal investigation into why a council officer was not fined for parking on double yellow lines, in the presence of traffic wardens.

It said it would be disproportionate and unfair to disclose the details of the investigation, as to do so would be unusual and it could be professionally detrimental to those involved.

The officer, who had middle management status, had a reasonable expectation of confidentiality.

It was relevant that the case had already attracted publicity because a video of the car parking incident was posted online.

(Information Tribunal, 2016, *Steve Pritchard and Information Commissioner EA/2015/0175.*)

In contrast, Bolton Council was ordered to name a councillor who failed to pay council tax, saying that the councillor would not be disproportionately prejudiced if the information was released.

It also said the public had a right know whether elected officials were fulfilling their duties, especially as failure to pay council tax can result in a councillor being disqualified from voting on a council's budget.

(BAILII, 2016, UKUT 139 (AAC).)

CHAPTER 6

COPYRIGHT

Online publishers often want to use other people's content and therefore should have a good knowledge of copyright laws.

Copyright is now more strictly enforced on the internet than it used to be, and publishers can expect to receive an invoice or a solicitor's letter if they use someone else's content without consent.

This is especially the case with images.

Copyright law is simple: if a person does not own the copyright, someone else does. And if a person wishes to use third-party content, they must usually get consent, credit the copyright owners, and possibly pay for the use.

Copyright is covered by the Copyright Designs and Patents Act (CDPA) 1998 (UK Legislation, n.d., *Copyright, Designs and Patents Act*), which has been amended by several EU directives.

Copyright law protects the products of people's skill, labour, creativity and time and is usually owned by the person who created a work, unless it was commissioned by someone else.

What Copyright Law Covers

Work must be 'fixed' in order for copyright to apply, that is: written down, recorded, filmed, inputted onto a PC, photographed, etc.

Copyright automatically applies to the following:

- Written content.

- Music.

- Photos, logos and graphics, even if they are modified to create a 'new' image.

- Audio recordings.

- Films, TV programmes and videos.

- Magazine or newspaper design: the fonts, colours, layout.

- Databases.

Copyright for written, dramatic, musical and artistic work, films and sound and music recording usually lasts for 70 years after the originator's death, no matter who owns the copyright.

It lasts 50 years for broadcasts.

What Copyright Law Does Not Cover

There is no copyright on news, facts, ideas or information. Copyright only applies to the way these are selected, arranged, and presented to create an original work.

However, the persistent lifting of facts from another publication, even if they are rewritten each time, may be seen as an infringement.

Who Owns Copyright

Copyright applies automatically; it does not have to be registered. However, there are varying arrangements for certain situations.

Freelance writers and photographers own the copyright to their work unless they have signed an agreement to the contrary.

Many newspapers and magazines commission work on the basis that the copyright belongs to them, and this can be very unpopular with freelancers, who stand to lose money by signing away their syndication rights.

Case Study

A ruling in 2015 by the Court of Justice of the European Union (CJEU) allows photographers to sue for copyright breaches in the UK courts, if their photos have been used in another EU country.

In the past, actions had to be brought in the country where the photos were published.

An Austrian photographer, Ms Pez Hejduk, brought a copyright claim in an Austrian court, claiming that a German company EnergieAgentur had used her photos on their website without consent.

The company said she should have brought the action in Germany, as their website was not aimed at the Austrian market.

However, the CJEU said that damage had occurred in Austria because Ms Hejduk's photos were accessible online there and that her copyright was protected by Austrian law.

The ruling may help UK photographers and publishers whose images are published on websites in other EU countries.

(InfoCuria – Case-law of the Court of Justice, 2015, *Pez Hejduk v EnergieAgentur*.)

People own the copyright to their letters published on newspaper and magazine letters' pages, but they license the publisher for one free use. This can extend to comments left on message boards.

Copyright can apply to the spoken word but speakers must assert their rights in writing, in advance. Speakers can also restrict who uses their words.

So someone may give a freelance journalist or blogger an interview on the condition that they can only sell it to the Daily Telegraph or the Daily Express.

However, these restrictions do not apply when people are speaking in the course of their employment or in speeches made in parliamentary or judicial proceedings.

Incidental breaches of copyright are allowed. For instance, if a photographer takes a photo of a man for a feature about his charity work, and it happens to include a copyrighted painting in the shot, his photos will be unlikely to breach the artist's copyright.

Images Taken with Mobile Phones

Many journalists and members of the public assume that copyright always applies to photos taken with smartphones.

In fact, the situation is less clear-cut following a judgment by the ECJ in the case of Eva-Maria Painer v Standard Verlags GmbH and Others in 2011.

The judges said that items like photos could be subject to copyright if they were 'original', in the sense that they are intellectual creations and that they show an element of creative skill.

In other words, that they reflect the author's personality, and that the author expressed their creative abilities by making free and creative choices when they took them.

(BAILII, 2011, C-145/10.)

It could be argued that photos taken with smartphones on the spur of the moment do not provide the author with the opportunity to express their creative abilities, and therefore are not automatically subject to copyright.

Also, the owner of a 'selfie' or similar 'snatch' photo may have difficulty arguing that the image involved the use of "skill, labour and time".

Fair Dealing

Fair dealing is a valuable tool for anyone who publishes on social media or the internet.

It is sometimes called 'fair use' (mainly in the US) and allows free use of substantial extracts of copyright work in certain circumstances, provided the copyright owner is given a suitable credit.

'Substantial' is usually taken to mean up to one-third of the original content but may also depend on the proportion the extract makes up in the new article.

The courts will also look at the extract's commercial value.

So if a small excerpt is taken from a short but highly specialised publication, this might be construed as an infringement.

Courts over the years have made it clear that 'substantial' can refer to quality or quantity.

Fair dealing covers:

- **Reports of current events**. Photos are not included.

  It allows publishers to use extracts of copyright work in order to report events contemporaneously and to report past events that are still genuinely newsworthy.

- **Private study or research for a non-commercial purpose**. However, research for an article to be published in a newspaper or a magazine is regarded as a commercial purpose, so fair dealing does not apply.

- **Criticism or review**. This includes extracts and photos from books, plays, films, and broadcasts to be included in a review.

  Online publishers should quote only as much material as they need to make their point.

- **Quotations**. This allows extracts from copyright works to be used to provide a 'quote' in the traditional sense of the word, but also to reference something that has already happened.

  For example, clips from various movies could be shown to illustrate the fact that a particular actor favours comedy roles.

- **Caricature, parody or pastiche**. This allows publishers to take an extract from a copyrighted work and build on it to create a separate 'mashed-up' work, usually for humorous effect.

  The IPO explains in its guidance, *Exceptions to Copyright – Guidance for Creators and Copyright Owners*: "A comedian may use a few lines from a film or song for a parody sketch; a cartoonist may reference a well-known artwork or illustration for a caricature; an artist may use small fragments from a range of films to compose a larger pastiche artwork" (GOV.UK, 2014, *Changes to Copyright Law*).

Case Study

There has been some uncertainty as to whether copyright applies to brief video clips used on apps like Periscope and animated gifs.

In March 2016, the High Court gave a partial answer in the case of England and Wales Cricket Board and Sky UK Limited v Tixdaq Limited and Fanatix Limited.

The case involved Fanatix's iOS app, which allowed users to upload, share and comment on short clips of sports footage.

Sky argued that these clips infringed their copyright, while the defendants said they counted as fair dealing (the reporting of current events).

Mr Justice Arnold had to decide whether eight-second clips constituted a 'substantial' part of the original broadcast which lasted up to two hours; and, if they did, whether they counted as fair dealing.

The judge ruled that the short clips were substantial, not in terms of quantity, but quality, as they showed the important highlights.

He also decided that they did not constitute fair dealing.

He said: "The clips were not used in order to inform the audience about a current event, but presented for consumption because of their intrinsic interest and value.

"Furthermore, although the fact that a news service is a commercial one funded by advertising revenue does not prevent its use from being for the purpose of reporting current events, I consider that the defendants' objective was purely commercial rather than genuinely informatory" (BAILII, 2016, EWHC 575).

The following two cases also illustrate how fair dealing can be contested.

Case Study

The Independent claimed 'no copyright in news', when it used a story which first appeared on Wales Online.

The court story – about a man who placed wire across a pathway used by cyclists – had been sold to the website by a freelance journalist.

The Independent used the story and inserted a hyperlink to Wales Online but refused to pay freelancer Glyn Bellis, when he was alerted to its publication.

A spokesman for the newspaper told the Press Gazette it had based its own report on that in Wales Online – which it credited – and owed nothing to Bellis.

(Ponsford, 2017, *Independent Declines to Pay for Court Story 'Lifted' From Wales Online Telling Freelance: 'There Is no Copyright in News'.*)

Case Study

The Manchester Evening News (MEN) was ordered to pay £200 to Rochdale Online after it used a story about a former town MP's expenses, which first appeared on the online news site.

The story was based on a Freedom of Information request submitted by Rochdale Online.

After it was used in the daily paper without credit, the MEN claimed 'no copyright in news' and apparently sold the story to the Sun.

The website took the paper to the small claims court and won £200 in damages.

For its part, the MEN said its article "did not copy any of Rochdale Online's words" (Ponsford, 2017, *'David and Goliath' Legal Battle Sees Rochdale Online Win Legal Battle from Manchester Evening News over Danczuk Expenses Story*).

Moral Rights

Anyone who commissions a photo from a freelancer or studio for private or domestic use has the right to veto publication, even if they do not own the copyright.

This means that people who 'borrow' photos or download them from social media platforms like Facebook should obtain copyright consent from the people who took the photos, in the usual way.

And, they should also obtain permission to publish them from the people who commissioned them, if the pictures have been professionally taken.

Copyright law also provides three other moral rights:

1. The right to be identified as the copyright owner.

2. The right not to have the work subject to derogatory treatment.

   This is defined as any addition, deletion, alteration to or adaptation of a work that amounts to a distortion or mutilation of the work, or is otherwise prejudicial to the honour or reputation of the author.

   However, this does not apply to work produced for the news media – presumably to prevent contributors from objecting to it being subjected to the ruthless skills of subeditors.

3. The right to object to false attribution. This prevents instances where, for example, a journalist has interviewed someone, and then used their quotes with a byline, implying that the speaker actually wrote the article.

Copyright Breaches

Most copyright disputes involving online publishers are dealt with by the Intellectual Property Enterprise Court's small claims track, which handles claims of up to £10,000.

The onus is on the copyright owner to prove that the work is original.

The copyright owner can:

- Obtain an injunction preventing further infringement.

- Obtain damages and costs.

- Obtain an order for the possession of the copyrighted work and any equipment used in the infringement.

- Force the defendant to account for the profits made from the infringement.

Copyright licensing disputes are handled by the Copyright Tribunal.

Case Study

In 2019, the High Court denied an interim injunction over copyright to a couple who claimed that a planned BBC comedy-drama exploited a script about the bequest of a caravan site which they had sent into the BBC three years earlier and which had been rejected for further development as a script.

The judge in the case said that any similarities between the two scripts were minor, that the injunction had only been sought the day before the broadcast, and that there was greater potential damage to the BBC in terms of cost and time wasted if the injunction were to be granted.

(BAILII, 2019, EWHC 558.)

Copyright Defences

The main copyright defences are:

- **Public interest**. This defence is unclear but may apply if there is a strong public interest in the copyrighted material.

- **Innocent infringement.** This applies if the infringer did not know, and had no reason to believe, that the work was subject to copyright; for example, they believed it had expired.

  Writers and freelance journalists are advised to use the copyright symbol with each article they write, as it prevents people from claiming that they did not know it was protected.

- **Consent**. This can either be express consent such as contract or agreement, or implied consent, judged according to the circumstances, correspondence, etc.

Online Content

Everyone owns their online content, including photos, videos, tweets, status updates on Facebook, LinkedIn and other social media websites, blogs, and comments they make on other people's websites.

However, when they sign up to social media channels such as Facebook, Tumblr, Flickr, Twitter, Instagram and YouTube, they give these websites the right to adapt, distribute and use their content in promotional material, worldwide.

With Twitter, this includes live streams using an app like Periscope.

For example, in its terms of use, Instagram says that anyone sharing images on its site thereby grants to them "a non-exclusive, royalty-free, transferable, sub-licensable, worldwide licence to host, use, distribute, modify, run, copy, publicly perform or display, translate, and create derivative works" of their content.

In this way, Instagram can profit commercially from a person's work for any posted images.

Instagram's terms of use can be seen here:

https://help.instagram.com/478745558852511

In 2016, Ed Vaizey, as minister for culture, media and sport, reminded social media users that taking and sharing screenshots of Snapchat images was a breach of copyright.

In an answer to a written question, he said: "Under UK copyright law, it would be unlawful for a Snapchat user to copy an image and make it available to the public without the consent of the image owner.

"The image owner would be able to sue anyone who does this for copyright infringement" (Vaizey, 2016, *Social Networking: Photographs*).

People who share screenshots via Snapchat, Twitter and other platforms may be able to defend themselves under the rules of fair dealing or claim that the copyright owner – who may not be the sender – gave implied copyright consent.

Snapchat photos are automatically deleted after 10 seconds.

The Snapchat privacy policy states that if Snapchat detects that a recipient has taken a screenshot of an image, they will try to inform the original poster.

However, Snapchat advises users to avoid sending messages that they would not want someone to save or share.

Mr Vaizey also warned that sharing private sexual photos or films can breach the Criminal Justice and Courts Act 2015.

For more information on this, see the section on Sexting under the heading *Online Abuse*

Web editors may face take-down requests under the Digital Economy Act (DEA) 2017, if an online visitor posts a photo belonging to someone else on a message board.

If a web editor receives a request, they should:

- Check that it is valid.

- Remove the photo.

- Give the contributor a written warning.

- Tell them where they can get the image legally.

- Record the details, as the copyright owner can also get a court order requiring the website to reveal the IP address owner's details.

Under the Act, the maximum sentence for online copyright infringement was increased from two to 10 years.

And a new online design registration system known as webmarking was created to make it easier for design owners to protect their rights.

Creative Commons License (CCL)

Many copyright owners allow other users to use their work under any one of six CCLs, which can be viewed here:

http://creativecommons.org/licenses/

This is a valuable facility for journalists and bloggers.

However, they should check the licence conditions before publishing any material, and adhere to the T&Cs.

They should also make sure that the T&Cs have not changed since the photo was originally made available.

Media law blogger David Banks issued a salutary warning about the use of Creative Commons, with a reminder that people should always correctly attribute copyright, or they may find themselves facing a hefty bill.

(Banks, D., 2019, *Image Copyright – Beware of the Bots.*)

It can be expensive to breach someone's copyright, especially if lifting photos from other websites or social media channels.

The perpetrator can be charged for the original images, plus damages and costs.

In 2015, Judge Richard Hacon ruled that a company that lifted photos from another site should pay the original licence fee of £300, plus the additional £6,000 because their actions were "flagrant".

The ruling under section 97 of the Copyright, Designs and Patents Act is not binding, as each case is different. But the case gives a useful pointer on how courts may deal with similar cases in the future.

It provided clarity about when additional damages are available to copyright owners on top of a notional licence fee. People who copy other people's photos on their websites should take note.

Some bloggers, journalists and marketers are prepared to gamble, hoping they will only have to pay the copyright licence fee if they are caught.

Judge Hacon's ruling means that illegally using other people's images can be expensive.

(BAILII, 2015, EWHC 2608 (IPEC).)

However, copyright laws do give some wriggle room.

Photos are only protected if taking them involved creative skill, labour and time. So as mentioned above, selfies and 'quick' photos taken on smartphones may not qualify.

In addition, journalists and bloggers can use photos copyright-free for reviewing things like books, films or music, if they credit the copyright owner.

But if they want pictures for their website, it's best to take their own photos or use a free site like Pixabay, Photopin or Unsplash.

There are some very convincing schemes (or scams) around, whereby people receive emails charging them for 'illicit' use of pictures on their website or blog.

Anyone receiving such emails should take advice before responding.

Copyright of Tweets

Tweets are unlikely to be long enough to receive protection under the CDPA, although this issue has not yet been dealt with by UK courts.

However, the ECJ decided, in the case of Infopaq International A/S v Danske Dagblades Forening, in 2011, that as few as 11 words qualify for protection, provided they are the "expression of the intellectual creation of its author" (EUR-Lex, 2012, *Infopaq International A/S v Danske Dagblades Forening*).

This means that copyright could apply if someone tweets or retweets:

- A short poem, like a haiku.

- An original saying or proverb.

- A poem, one line at a time.

The ECJ has left it to national courts to decide their stance in each case.

In 2012, Twitter changed its procedures for copyright complaints made under the US Digital Millennium Copyright Act (DMCA) 1998.

Twitter now 'withholds' the tweets, and posts its own tweet explaining why the 'offensive' tweet no longer appears.

It used to simply remove them, leaving people wondering why they had been taken down.

Case Study

In 2017, a freelancer photographer attempted to sue Sky News after it used an embedded tweet containing one of his images.

Eddie Mitchell had allowed Midhurst Fire Service to use the image of a hotel fire in Bognor Regis in a tweet from the fire service account, and this was subsequently used by Sky in an online article about the fire.

The tweet was removed after Mitchell complained but Sky News lawyers told him the fact that the tweet containing the image was freely available via an embed meant there was no breach of copyright.

(Mayhew, 2017, *Freelance Photographer Sues Sky News after it Refuses to Pay for Image Used in Embedded Twitter Message*.)

Copyright and Pinterest

Online publishers face two contrasting issues with the virtual pinboard site Pinterest.

First, they should get consent before publishing other people's images. Second, they should monitor the site for illegal uses of their own images.

Pinterest has different T&Cs from Facebook and similar sites.

Account holders are responsible for checking the copyright of everything they post, as well as for the full cost of any legal action that could follow.

This includes actions against Pinterest's owners, Cold Brew Labs. In reality, however, few users check copyright before they pin.

The website differs from Google image results because Google does not actually store copies of the images it displays, whereas Pinterest does.

It is also different from social media sites, which just display a thumbnail of the image, with a link back to the source.

Pinterest stores a full-size copy of each image and allows visitors to re-pin images on their own pages, thus facilitating further copyright breaches.

However, it does not take responsibility for copyright breaches. Its T&Cs place the liability with the person who made the pin.

However, Pinterest will remove copyright images on request.

Some people are happy to allow extracts from their publications to be 'pinned'.

Others opt to use a special code on their images, which prevents them from being copied to Pinterest.

New EU Copyright Directive

In 2019, the EU Parliament passed the new Directive on Copyright in the Digital Single Market, which signalled major changes to copyright law and was passed only in the face of fierce opposition from internet giants such as Google and YouTube.

Although the law will take as long as two years to be implemented in member states, social media platforms argue that two key parts of the directive – Articles 11 and

13 – will have a significant impact on their ability to perform as profitable businesses.

Why are they so worried? Article 13 (confusingly, now officially Article 17) says that online content-sharing platforms such as YouTube should be legally forced to consider the IP rights of musicians, for example, who have their videos uploaded without consent and who receive no royalty payment in return.

Platforms will be forced to issue a notice to anyone who uploads copyright-protected works without permission.

Liability for copyright infringement will rest with online platforms, which will be expected to introduce 'upload filters'.

Online platforms will be exempt from action if they can show they have made 'best efforts' to 'expeditiously' remove protected work when alerted to it, or to make it unavailable.

There will be no infringement if permission is given for the content to be uploaded.

Smaller organisations will have a lighter touch placed on them by the new directive, which takes into account the cost and resource implications for implementing Article 13.

Exemptions apply to parodies, pastiches, works of criticism, etc.

Article 11 – which has become known as the 'link tax' – concerns hyperlinking and aggregation of news.

Under the new directive, online sites such as Google News and Facebook have to pay a licence fee for publishing links to content created by publishers such as news organisations.

Google News, in particular, has been vocal in its criticism of Article 11, with threats to close down its operations, and arguing that it performs a vital function in sending audiences to news platforms through its linking.

Google claims it has already seen a 45% decrease in news traffic due to the effects of Article 11.

But the move is an acknowledgment that Google and other platforms have profited from the trade in news on the web, while publishers such as news platforms have not reaped the same, if any, commercial rewards.

The passing of the directive was hailed as a "historic vote" by Carlo Perrone, president of the European Newspaper Publishers' Association, who said it was "essential for the future of press publishing and professional journalism" (Mayhew, 2019, *European Publishers Welcome New Digital Copyright Directive Passed by EU Parliament*).

The 'link tax' is potentially great news for online news publishers who work hard to produce content only to see internet giants boost their profits by aggregating their news output on their platforms.

Article 11 refers to the banning of links to anything more than 'brief snippets', but commentators have quite rightly pointed out that this leaves room for ambiguity. Is it one or two words or a paragraph? Only test cases will decide that.

(Mayhew, 2019, *New EU Copyright Deal Will Allow Facebook and Google to Share 'Very Short' News Snippets Only.*)

Full details of the EU Copyright Directive can be found here:

https://eur-lex.europa.eu/legal-content/EN/TXT/?uri=COM:2016:0593:FIN

The CJEU has been asked to consider a case of copyright infringement after a YouTube user uploaded two films to the site without permission from the creators.

The company involved requested the IP address and other details of the uploader.

The German Federal Court ruled that YouTube should supply the email address but was not under any obligation to provide an IP address or phone number.

It will be interesting to see how the CJEU interprets this judgment.

(Lexology, 2019, How Much Information is Enough Information? CJEU Asked to Rule on the Extent of Online Platforms' Responsibility to Copyright Holders.)

TRADEMARKS

The Law

Trademarks were protected under the Trademark Act 1994 (until March 2016).

The Act is still in force, but was superseded by the EU Trademarks Directive, which aimed to harmonise trademark law across the EU.

It remains to be seen what effect Brexit will have on the law, but it is unlikely the directive will result in significant changes for journalists and other online publishers.

Trademarks are Important

Most companies guard trademarks ferociously. They are valuable commodities, and businesses spend millions to distinguish them from their rivals. They will not tolerate any breaches.

Case Study

A company called Panini Cheapskates received a trademark infringement notice from Manchester United after it produced a series of 'wonky' stickers depicting various team players.

The firm, which was created as an easier alternative to the official Panini albums, was told by United it had breached its IP rights by featuring ex-players in their collection.

Interestingly, legal opinion states that while parody versions of others' work are acceptable in copyright under fair use, no such right exists in trademarks.

(Lexology, 2019, *Panini Cheapskates: Straight Infringement for a 'Wonky Parody'*.)

Case Study

In 2019, internationally renowned graffiti artist Banksy successfully sued Mudec Museum in Milan for infringing his trademarks by selling unauthorised merchandise, which a judge ruled had to be removed from the museum's gift shop.

More than one commentator remarked on the irony of Banksy – who once described copyright as being "for losers" – pursuing his case.

(Bonadio, 2019, *Banksy Finally Goes to Court to Stop Unauthorised Merchandising, Despite Saying Copyright Is for Losers.*)

Once a trademark starts to be used as a noun or verb, there is a real risk that its distinctiveness will be eroded, diluted or even lost entirely.

And when that happens, the trademark may be revoked because it has become generic.

This means a trademark becomes synonymous with all products of its kind. For example, people say they are 'doing the hoovering', even if they are using a Dyson or a Vax.

Businesses do not want their products lumped together with all the others.

Anyone using trademarks incorrectly can expect to receive letters of complaint from the businesses that own the trademarks, followed by court action if the mistakes are not rectified.

Because trademarks are valuable, businesses want to keep them distinctive. Online publishers should, therefore:

- Check for registration of trademarked words and images on the IPO website.

  (GOV.UK, n.d., *Intellectual Property Office*.)

- Use trademarks correctly and use the ® symbol if the trademark is registered.

- Use generic words instead of trademarked words, to avoid a complaint. For instance, it would be better to refer to 'painkillers' than 'Aspirin'.

Check for Trademark Registration

The easiest way to check whether words are trademarks is to use the IPO website:

http://www.ipo.gov.uk/types/tm/t-os/t-find.htm

However, this is not an exhaustive list.

Some trademarks are registered on a 'word only' basis.

This means that only the pure text is trademarked; others are trademarked as 'stylised words', which are used as part of a logo or written only in a specific typeface.

When referring to protected company or product names, the term to use is 'trademark'. The terms 'copyright' or 'patent-protected' are different and not related to trademark law.

How to Use Trademarks Correctly

It is important to not only check whether a word is a trademark but to also make sure that the item being referred to was made by that company, and not another.

For example, if a portable cabin is not made by Portakabin, it must simply be called a portable cabin, and not a Portakabin.

Aspirin, Sellotape and escalator are all trademarks but have been absorbed into the language as generic terms. So have portacabins and google.

This does not mean that these generic terms can be used in copy.

Therefore, a reference to someone 'doing the hoovering' should be changed to someone 'doing the vacuuming with a Hoover® vacuum cleaner'.

It is also a good idea to check whether using the trademarked name is important in context. It might be sufficient to say: 'used a paper tissue', rather than saying: 'used a Kleenex® tissue', unless the trademark is important to the story.

How to Write Trademarks

Trademarks should:

- Be spelled correctly, eg, Portakabin, not Portacabin.

- Be capitalised appropriately, eg, Kleenex, not kleenex.

- Be used as an adjective followed by the appropriate noun, eg: 'wiped with a Kleenex® tissue', not 'wiped with a Kleenex®'.

- Be followed by the ® symbol if they are registered; not all trademarks are registered. The term TM means nothing in the UK.

- Never be pluralised, eg: 'Jiffies'.

- Never be used in the possessive form, eg: 'Kleenex's tissues'.

- Never be used as verbs, eg: 'I am going to google it.'

Some companies are not too bothered about affixing the ® symbol when they write their own trademarks, whereas others are very explicit about its use. For example, Kleenex® uses the ® symbol in certain contexts but not in others.

And some publications and websites do not use the ® symbol after registered trademarks. However, anyone in doubt should follow the law.

For more details on trademarks, see:

http://www.ipo.gov.uk/types/tm/t-manage/t-enforce.htm

Hashtags

Is it possible to trademark a hashtag? The presence of a hash sign # in front of a word or phrase makes no difference in law. Only the trademarked word(s) are protected.

Whether this means that the use of someone's hashtag by another person is an infringement of their trademark is another matter.

The law is not particularly clear on the issue, with contradictory decisions being made by the courts.

The key message from legal opinion is to tread with caution where marks and hashtags are concerned.

CHAPTER 7

DEALING WITH HYPERLINKS

There used to be a time when websites welcomed inbound links.

However, many websites now threaten legal action in order to prevent their content from being accessed by an unauthorised link.

Most web users believe that website operators automatically give implied consent for people to link to any page they publish. But this is not always the case – especially when there's money to be made.

For instance, a link may bypass a paywall, or try to exploit a commercial advantage from another page.

Case Study

One of the earliest cases on unauthorised linking was that of Shetland Times v Wills.

(Net Litigation, 1996, *Shetland Times, Ltd. v Dr Jonathan Wills and Another.*)

From October 1996, the Shetland News website reproduced several news headlines from their rival publication, the Shetland Times.

The Shetland News also hyperlinked these headlines to the Shetland Times webpages.

The Shetland Times argued that the Shetland News was breaching the CDPA by passing off Shetland Times stories as their own and won an interim injunction at the Court of Session, Edinburgh, to stop this practice.

Lord Hamilton said: "We all know that the homepage is the most popular area of a website. It is the gateway to the rest of the site.

"However, the ability to bypass the homepage and link directly to a certain webpage is surely fundamental to the continued success of the internet.

"Indeed, entire businesses have been created by indexing individual pages" (BBC News, 1997, *Shetland Internet Squabble Settled out of Court*).

The two parties eventually made a settlement, and the Shetland News agreed to acknowledge the ownership of any Shetland Times story which appeared on its website.

The practice of acknowledging the ownership of hyperlinks is still a good way to avoid legal problems.

Generally, linking deep into a website (such as linking to this webpage: *www.examplewebsite.com/products/ /hoses/parts/*) is more legally risky than simply linking to a homepage, eg: *www.examplewebsite.com*

However, web editors should be aware that any link to another website can present legal risks.

Other legal dangers associated with hyperlinks are discussed below.

Libel

Web editors should always check carefully before linking to defamatory content on other websites.

In the Islam Expo case referred to below, the Spectator and the Jewish Chronicle both paid damages and apologised after publishing a hyperlink to a libellous article.

A key point to arise from the case was that hyperlinking to defamatory material can lead to an action without the wider context of the article needing to be considered. The mere act of hyperlinking can be a cause for action.

Reporting that a news organisation is being sued for libel is safe enough, but publishing the offending article, or even providing a link to it, can be problematic.

Case Study

The legal precedent for linking to a defamatory article on another site is based on a case that goes back more than 100 years to 1894.

A man named Mr Wood sat by the side of a road pointing to a placard containing a defamatory statement about another man, Mr Hird.

It is unclear who wrote the statement. However, Hird sued Wood for libel, and the Court of Appeal decided that Wood was liable for publishing the statement because he had drawn attention to it.

(Defamation Update, n.d., *The Solicitors Journal/Cases of the Week/Hird v Wood*.)

This created the precedent that if publishers 'point' readers to defamatory content, they may share legal responsibility as a publisher.

The Hird v Wood case was referred to in the 2010 libel case Spectator and Islam Expo.

(BAILII, 2010/2011, EWHC 1828.)

In a preliminary hearing, Mr Justice Tugendhat ruled that content accessed via links in an article in the Spectator should be treated as part of the offending article in the trial.

There are other subtleties involved in the Hirst v Wood case that help to inform web editors.

First, Wood actively encouraged people to read the sign, and obviously approved of the statement.

In addition, he was situated in the same place as the placard.

Therefore, a hyperlink may be safe if it neither encourages people to read the page that it links to nor suggests that the website agrees with the content.

And it may also be possible to argue that another website is not in the same place as the original site.

Example

Linking to a defamatory article about 'celebrity' Jason Dipstick on the Sun's website may be safe because it lists the link without giving clues about the content of the Sun's article, and it does not actively encourage people to click.

For example, this may be safe:

> See News from Today's Sun

Whereas *this* link would be riskier because it gives clues about the content and encourages people to click:

> Who's a naughty boy then? Read about Jason Dipstick's Latest Exploits

Contempt of Court

Linking to an article on another website, even one based overseas, could prejudice someone's trial if proceedings were active, under the CoCA 1981.

Because contempt by publication is a strict liability offence, it may be harder for web editors to argue that they were not responsible for any contempt.

Publishers should beware of creating links from articles on a Scottish website to prejudicial stories on an English one, as contempt laws are applied more strictly in Scotland.

However, it would be safe to place a link, on a foreign website, to a story on a UK website about a person standing trial abroad.

Hyperlinks to sites that breach an injunction or a reporting restriction may also be seen as contempt of court.

Copyright

Generally, it is safe for the media to hyperlink to copyrighted material freely available online.

The courts have ruled that this does not constitute what in copyright law is referred to as a "communication to the public", and therefore will not be subject to action.

(Taylor Wessing, 2019, CJEU Rules that Knowingly Linking to Illegal Content Infringes Copyright.)

This general right extends to framing and embedding material such as tweets and videos from social media.

If the material is freely available online, with an option to embed or share, then consent for use is implied (see the *Sky News case*). The image is itself still subject to copyright but its use within a tweet is safe.

A similar case was heard in Germany when a company's video on water pollution was viewable on YouTube via a link from another company's website.

BestWater International sued Michael Mebes and Stefan Potsch for publishing the link, but judges ruled that the framing was not a communication to a new public and did not infringe copyright.

(EUR-Lex, 2014, *BestWater International GmbH v Michael Mebes, Stefan Potsch.*)

However, this ruling does not extend to material behind a paywall or which has been uploaded to the web illegally, ie without permission of the copyright holder. In this case, the act of embedding, hyperlinking or framing is not safe.

The ruling by the ECJ in 2016 in the following case study, reinforces this principle.

Case Study

The decision in the case of GS Media BV v Sanoma Media Netherlands BV effectively creates a new form of copyright infringement.

In October 2011, a Dutch website, GeenStijl, posted links to leaked photos from the Dutch version of Playboy.

Playboy's publishers, Sanoma Media, repeatedly asked for the links to be removed and eventually sued GeenStijl and its parent company, GS Media, for a breach of copyright.

The court agreed, as the website profited from the traffic that it generated.

GeenStijl lost its argument that the ruling reduced their ability to report newsworthy information.

The ruling is binding on all EU member states and means that posting hyperlinks to copyright work published illegally on third-party sites, as a commercial activity may be seen as a breach of copyright.

Although it cannot always be known whether material has been illegally uploaded, the law states that the onus is on the publisher to make the 'necessary checks', whether the material is freely available online or whether it has been uploaded illegally and/or behind a paywall.

This means that website operators will have to check each hyperlink to make sure it does not lead to content that infringes copyright, and remove links quickly if they receive a take-down request.

This legal obligation is particularly pertinent for websites that operate on a commercial basis.

Blogs and not-for-profit sites will not be in breach unless they know material has been uploaded illegally.

The GS Media ruling particularly affects media and news-oriented sites, which use links within articles and other content.

Some publishers may feel it is not worth spending the time and money on checking each link and responding to additional take-down requests.

The judges said in their ruling: "[...] it is undisputed that GS Media provided the hyperlinks to the files containing the photos for profit and that Sanoma had not authorised the publication of those photos on the internet."

They accepted that hyperlinks were integral to the internet and its benefits for free information and expression, and that regular internet users may find it difficult to check whether they are posting links to authorised or unauthorised material.

However, they added: "In contrast, where it is established that such a person knew or ought to have known that the hyperlink he posted provides access to a work illegally published, for example, because he was notified thereof by the copyright holders, the provision of that link constitutes a 'communication to the public'.

"Furthermore, when hyperlinks are posted for profit, it may be expected that the person who posted such a link should carry out the checks necessary to ensure that the work concerned is not illegally published."

See the court's statement here:

https://curia.europa.eu/jcms/upload/docs/application/pdf/2016-09/cp160092en.pdf

(InfoCuria – Case-law of the Court of Justice, 2016, *Case C-160/15 GS Media BV v Sanoma Media Netherlands BV, Playboy Enterprises International Inc., Britt Geertruida Dekker*.)

The ruling above overturned a decision in a previous case, Svensson and others v Retriever Sverige AB in 2014.

This involved four Swedish journalists who lost their case against a media monitoring and aggregation service, which provided links to their articles that had been published on other websites.

(5RB, n.d., *Nils Svensson and Others v Retriever Sverige AB.*)

Trademarks

If a trademark is used in a link, the link text should include the ® symbol if the trademark is registered.

Other Risks

Links to unlawful content that breaches privacy or confidentiality, incites racial or religious hatred, is obscene, or encourages or induces acts of terrorism could also risk prosecution, although it must be stressed there are no legal precedents.

In all these above instances, web editors will be more likely to face prosecution if:

- The main purpose of a link is to refer readers to the unlawful material.

- They know that the content they are linking to is unlawful.
- They actively refer people to the link.

However, a link created automatically by a website tool is unlikely to create any legal danger.

Mobile Journalism and the Terrorism Act 2000

Several photographers and video journalists taking footage in public places have been confronted by police officers requesting that they stop taking photos, and in some cases, officers have attempted to confiscate equipment under section 44 of the Terrorism Act 2000.

(UK Legislation, n.d., *Terrorism Act 2000.*)

In July 2010, section 44 was officially suspended, but if journalists plan to take photos or video footage in a public place, they should be aware of their rights, which are listed on this website:

http://media.gn.apc.org/photo/guidelines.html

Another useful website is 'I'm a Photographer, Not a Terrorist!', which includes a 'bust card' for journalists on this webpage: *http://phnat.org/bust-card/*

It explains what journalists should do if stopped by police in such circumstances.

APPENDIX

ABBREVIATIONS

ACTS AND REGULATIONS	
CA	Communications Act
CoCA	Contempt of Court Act
CDPA	Copyright Designs and Patents Act
CJA	Criminal Justice Act
CMA	Computer Misuse Act
DA	Defamation Act
DEA	Digital Economy Act
DMCA	US Digital Millennium Copyright Act
DPA	Data Protection Act
EDA	Education Act
EIR	Environmental Information Regulations
EPR	ePrivacy Regulation
FA	Fraud Act
FOIA	Freedom of Information Act
GDPR	General Data Protection Regulation
IPA	Investigatory Powers Act
PCA	Protection of Children Act
PHA	Protection from Harassment Act
RIPA	Regulation of Investigatory Powers Act
ROA	Rehabilitation of Offenders Act
SCA	Serious Crime Act
SOA	Sexual Offences Act
YJCEA	Youth Justice and Criminal Evidence Act

COURTS AND BODIES	
CJEU	Court of Justice of the European Union
EC	European Commission
ECHR	European Convention on Human Rights
ECJ	European Court of Justice (The court of the CJEU)
ECtHR	European Court of Human Rights
ECD	EU Electronic Commerce Directive
ICO	Information Commissioner's Office
IT	Information Tribunal
IPO	Intellectual Property Office
Ipso	Independent Press Standards Organisation (prev. PPC)
MoJ	Ministry of Justice

OTHER	
AG	Attorney General
CAA	Civil Aviation Authority
CCL	Creative Commons Licence
FGM	Female Genital Mutilation
IM	Instant messages
IP	Internet Protocol
MEN	Manchester Evening News
Ofcom code	Ofcom Broadcasting Code
T&Cs	Terms and Conditions
UGC	User-Generated Content

REFERENCE LIST

5RB (n.d.) *Flood v Times Newspapers Limited* [Online]. Available at
http://www.5rb.com/case/flood-v-times-newspapers-limited-sc/
(Accessed 25 August 2015).

5RB (n.d.) *Google Spain SL v Agencia Española de Protección de Datos*
[Online]. Available at *http://www.5rb.com/case/google-spain-sl-v-agencia-espanola-de-proteccion-de-datos/* (Accessed 21 August 2015).

5RB (n.d.) *Nils Svensson and Others v Retriever Sverige AB* [Online].
Available at *http://www.5rb.com/case/nils-svensson-others-v-retriever-sverige-ab/* (Accessed 25 August 2015).

BAILII (2002) EWHC 1600 (2002) *England and Wales High Court
(Queen's Bench Division) Decisions >> Lillie & Anor v Newcastle City
Council & Ors [2002] EWHC 1600(2) (QB) (30 July 2002)* [Online].
Available at
http://www.bailii.org/ew/cases/EWHC/QB/2002/1600(2).html
(Accessed 4 January 2017).

BAILII (2006) EWHC 90070 (SCCO) *England and Wales High Court
(Senior Courts Costs Office) Decisions >> Cole v News Group Newspapers
Ltd [2006] EWHC 90070 (Costs) (18 October 2006)* [Online]. Available
at *https://www.bailii.org/ew/cases/EWHC/Costs/2006/90070.html*
(Accessed 9 August 2019).

BAILII (2010) EWHC 2011 (2010) *England and Wales High Court
(Queen's Bench Division) Decisions Islam Expo Ltd v The Spectator (1828)
Ltd & Anor [2010] EWHC 2011 (QB) (30 July 2010)* [Online].
Available at
http://www.bailii.org/ew/cases/EWHC/QB/2010/2011.html
(Accessed 13 April 2016).

BAILII (2010/2011) EWHC 1828 *England and Wales High Court (Chancery Division) Decisions >> Alstom Transport v Eurostar International Ltd & Anor (Rev 1) [2011] EWHC 1828 (Ch) (13 July 2011)* [Online]. Available at
http://www.bailii.org/ew/cases/EWHC/Ch/2011/1828.html
(Accessed 9 August 2019).

BAILII (2011) C145/10 (2011) *Court of Justice of the European Communities (Including Court of First Instance Decisions) Painer v Standard Verlags GmbH (Area of Freedom, Security and Justice) [2011] EUECJ C-145/10 (12 April 2011)* [Online]. Available at
http://www.bailii.org/eu/cases/EUECJ/2011/C14510_O.html
(Accessed 24 March 2016).

BAILII (2012) EWHC 2981 (2012) *England and Wales High Court (Administrative Court) Decisions: Attorney General v Associated Newspapers Ltd & Anor EWHC 2981 [2012] (Admin) (16 October 2012)* [Online.] Available at
http://www.bailii.org/ew/cases/EWHC/Admin/2012/2981.html
(Accessed 18 March 2016).

BAILII (2012) EWHC 558 (Ch) *England and Wales High Court (Chancery Division) Decisions >> Happy Camper Productions Ltd v British Broadcasting Corporation (BBC) [2019] EWHC 558 (Ch) (11 February 2019)* [Online]. Available at
http://www.bailii.org/ew/cases/EWHC/Ch/2019/558.html
(Accessed 9 August 2019).

BAILII (2012) UKSC 11 (2012) *United Kingdom Supreme Court Judgment: Flood v Times Newspapers Ltd UKSC 11 [2012] (21 March 2012)* [Online.] Available at
https://www.bailii.org/uk/cases/UKSC/2012/11.html
(Accessed 17 March 2016).

BAILII (2013) ECHR 941 (2013) *European Court of Human Rights Chamber Judgment: Delfi AS v Estonia ECHR 941 [2013] (10 October 2013)* [Online.] Available at
http://www.bailii.org/eu/cases/ECHR/2013/941.html
(Accessed 18 March 2016).

BAILII (2013) EWHC 1342 (QB) *England and Wales High Court (Queen's Bench Division) Decisions >> McAlpine v Bercow [2013] EWHC 1342 (QB) (24 May 2013)* [Online]. Available at https://www.bailii.org/ew/cases/EWHC/QB/2013/1342.html (Accessed 9 August 2019).

BAILII (2014) EWHC 3349 (QB).

BAILII (2015) ECHR 586 (2015) *European Court of Human Rights Grand Chamber Judgment: Delfi AS v Estonia ECHR 586 [2015] (16 June 2015)* [Online.] Available at http://www.bailii.org/eu/cases/ECHR/2015/586.html (Accessed 18 March 2016).

BAILII (2015) EWHC 2608 (IPEC) *Intellectual Property Enterprise Court >> Absolute Lofts South West London Ltd v Artisan Home Improvements Ltd & Anor [2015] EWHC 2608 (IPEC) (14 September 2015).* [Online]. Available at https://www.bailii.org/ew/cases/EWHC/IPEC/2015/2608.html (Accessed 9 August 2019).

BAILII (2015) EWHC 2628 *England and Wales High Court (Queen's Bench Division) Decisions >> Brett Wilson LLP v Person(s) Unknown, Responsible for the Operation and Publication of the Website www.solicitorsfromhelluk.com [2015] EWHC 2628 (QB) (16 September 2015)* [Online]. Available at https://www.bailii.org/ew/cases/EWHC/QB/2015/2628.html (Accessed 9 August 2019).

BAILII (2015) EWHC 3380 (2015) *England and Wales High Court (Queen's Bench Division) Decisions: Ahuja v Politika Novine I Magazini D.O.O & Ors EWHC 3380 [2015] (QB) (23 November 2015)* [Online.] Available at http://www.bailii.org/ew/cases/EWHC/QB/2015/3380.html (Accessed 4 April 2016).

BAILII (2015) EWHC 3769 *England and Wales High Court (Queen's Bench Division) Decisions: Theedom v Nourish Training (t/a Recruitment Colin Sewell) EWHC 3769 [2015] (QB) (11 December 2015)* [Online] Available at
http://www.bailii.org/ew/cases/EWHC/QB/2015/3769.html
(Accessed 16 March 2016).

BAILII (2016) ECHR 135 (2016) *European Court of Human Rights Judgment: Magyar Tartalomszolgaltatok Egyesulete and Index.Hu Zrt v Hungary ECHR 135 [2016] (02 February 2016)* [Online.] Available at
http://www.bailii.org/eu/cases/ECHR/2016/135.html
(Accessed 18 March 2016).

BAILII (2016) EWCA Civ 100 (2016) *England and Wales Court of Appeal (Civil Division) Decisions PJS v News Group Newspapers Ltd [2016] EWCA Civ 100 (22 January 2016)* [Online]. Available at
http://www.bailii.org/ew/cases/EWCA/Civ/2016/100.html
(Accessed 13 April 2016).

BAILII (2016) EWHC 183 (2016) *England and Wales High Court (Administrative Court) Decisions: Ewing v Crown Court Sitting at Cardiff & Newport & Ors [2016] EWHC 183 (Admin) (08 February 2016* [Online.] Available at
http://www.bailii.org/ew/cases/EWHC/Admin/2016/183.html
(Accessed 18 March 2016).

BAILII (2016) EWHC 3295 (Ch) *England and Wales High Court (Chancery Division) Decisions >> A & B v Persons Unknown [2016] EWHC 3295 (Ch) (19 December 2016)* [Online]. Available at
https://www.bailii.org/ew/cases/EWHC/Ch/2016/3295.html
(Accessed 9 August 2019).

BAILII (2016) EWHC 575 (2016) *England and Wales High Court (Chancery Division) Decisions England and Wales Cricket Board Ltd & Anor v Tixdaq Ltd & Anor [2016] EWHC 575 (Ch) (18 March 2016)* [Online]. Available at
http://www.bailii.org/ew/cases/EWHC/Ch/2016/575.html
(Accessed 30 March 2016).

BAILII (2016) UKUT 139 (AAC) *Upper Tribunal (Administrative Appeals Chamber) >> DH v Information Commissioner & Anor (Information Rights: Freedom of Information – Absolute Exemptions) [2016] UKUT 139 (AAC) (10 March 2016)* [Online]. Available at *https://www.bailii.org/uk/cases/UKUT/AAC/2016/139.html* (Accessed 9 August 2019).

BAILII (2017) EWCA Civ 1334 *England and Wales Court of Appeal (Civil Division) Decisions >> Lachaux v Independent Print Ltd [2017] EWCA Civ 1334 (12 September 2017)* [Online]. Available at *https://www.bailii.org/ew/cases/EWCA/Civ/2017/1334.html* (Accessed 13 August 2019).

BAILII (2018) EWHC 1570 *England and Wales High Court (Queen's Bench Division) Decisions >> Burki v Seventy Thirty Ltd & Ors [2018] EWHC 1570 (QB) (21 June 2018)* [Online]. Available at *http://www.bailii.org/ew/cases/EWHC/QB/2018/1570.html* (Accessed 9 August 2019).

BAILII (2018) EWHC 1725 (QB) *England and Wales High Court (Queen's Bench Division) Decisions: Morgan v Associated Newspapers Ltd [2018] EWHC 1850 (QB) (28 June 2018)* [Online]. Available at *https://www.bailii.org/ew/cases/EWHC/QB/2018/1850.html* (Accessed 9 August 2019).

BAILII (2018) EWHC 2935 *England and Wales High Court (Queen's Bench Division) Decisions >> Doyle v Smith [2018] (QB) (02 November 2018)* [Online]. Available at *https://www.bailii.org/ew/cases/EWHC/QB/2018/2935.html* (Accessed 9 August 2019).

BAILII (2019) ECHR 221 *European Court of Human Rights >> HØINESS v NORWAY – 43624/14 (Judgment : No Article 8 – Right to Respect for Private and Family Life : Second Section) [2019] ECHR 221 (19 March 2019)* [Online]. Available at *http://www.bailii.org/eu/cases/ECHR/2019/221.html* (Accessed 9 August 2019).

BAILII (2019) EWHC 1413 *England and Wales High Court (Queen's Bench Division) Decisions >> Alsaifi v Secretary of State for Education [2019] EWHC 1413 (QB) (06 June 2019)* [Online]. Available at *https://www.bailii.org/ew/cases/EWHC/QB/2019/1413.html* (Accessed 9 August 2019).

BAILII (2019) EWHC 1469 (QB) *England and Wales High Court (Queen's Bench Division) Decisions: Advertising Standards Authority Ltd v Mitchell [2019] EWHC 1469 (QB) (11 June 2019)* [Online]. Available at *https://www.bailii.org/ew/cases/EWHC/QB/2019/1469.html* (Accessed 9 August 2019).

BAILII (2019) EWHC 1791 *England and Wales High Court (Queen's Bench Division) Decisions >> HM Attorney General v Yaxley-Lennon (Rev 1) [2019] EWHC 1791 (QB) (09 July 2019)* [Online]. Available at *https://www.bailii.org/ew/cases/EWHC/QB/2019/1791.html* (Accessed 9 August 2019).

BAILII (2019) EWHC 2026 (QB) *England and Wales High Court (Queen's Bench Division) Decisions >> RXG v Ministry of Justice & Ors [2019] EWHC 2026 (QB) (29 July 2019)* [Online]. Available at *https://www.bailii.org/ew/cases/EWHC/QB/2019/2026.html* (Accessed 13 August 2019).

BAILII (2019) EWHC 396 (QB) *England and Wales High Court (Queen's Bench Division) Decisions >> Suttle v Walker [2019] EWHC 396 (QB) (18 January 2019)* [Online]. Available at *https://www.bailii.org/ew/cases/EWHC/QB/2019/396.html* (Accessed 9 August 2019).

BAILII (2019) EWHC, QB, 1439 *England and Wales High Court (Queen's Bench Division) Decisions >> Spicer v The Commissioner of Police of the Metropolis [2019] EWHC 1439 (QB) (07 June 2019)* [Online]. Available at *https://www.bailii.org/ew/cases/EWHC/QB/2019/1439.html* (Accessed 9 August 2019).

BAILII (2019) UKSC 17 *United Kingdom Supreme Court >> Stocker v Stocker [2019] UKSC 17 (3 April 2019)* [Online]. Available at *https://www.bailii.org/uk/cases/UKSC/2019/17.html* (Accessed 9 August 2019).

BAILII (2019) UKSC 27 *United Kingdom Supreme Court >> Lachaux v Independent Print Ltd & Anor [2019] UKSC 27 (12 June 2019)* [Online]. Available at *https://www.bailii.org/uk/cases/UKSC/2019/27.html* (Accessed 13 August 2019).

BAILLI (2018) EWHC 3525 *England and Wales High Court (Queen's Bench Division) Decisions >> Monir v Wood [2018] EWHC 3525 (QB) (19 December 2018)* [Online]. Available at *https://www.bailii.org/ew/cases/EWHC/QB/2018/3525.html* (Accessed 9 August 2019).

BAILLI (2019) EWHC 893 *England and Wales High Court (Queen's Bench Division) Decisions >> Rudd v Bridle & Anor (Rev 1) [2019] EWHC 893 (QB) (10 April 2019)* [Online]. Available at *https://www.bailii.org/ew/cases/EWHC/QB/2019/893.html* (Accessed 9 August 2019).

Banks, D (2019) *Image Copyright – Beware of the Bots* [Online]. Available at *https://davidbanksmedialaw.com/2019/06/04/image-copyright-beware-of-the-bots/* (Accessed 5 June 2019).

BBC News (1997) *Shetland Internet Squabble Settled out of Court* [Online]. Available at *http://news.bbc.co.uk/1/hi/sci/tech/29191.stm* (Accessed 20 April 2016).

BBC News (2010) *Edlington Attack 'Could Have Been Prevented')* [Online]. Available at *http://news.bbc.co.uk/1/mobile/programmes/newsnight/8459938.stm* (Accessed 5 January 2017).

BBC News (2018) *Abdulrahman Alcharbati Jailed for Terrorism Facebook Videos* [Online]. Available at *https://www.bbc.co.uk/news/uk-england-tyne-46572933* (Accessed 25 March 2019).

BBC News (2018) *Britain First Leader and Deputy Leader Jailed for Hate Crimes* [Online]. Available at *https://www.bbc.co.uk/news/uk-england-43320121* (Accessed 20 March 2019).

BBC News (2018) *Stoke-on-Trent Central Candidate Jailed for Race Hate Crimes* [Online]. Available at *https://www.bbc.co.uk/news/uk-england-stoke-staffordshire-45760727* (Accessed 20 March 2019).

BBC News (2019) *Alesha MacPhail Murder: Judge Lifts Ban on Naming Killer Aaron Campbell* [Online]. Available at *https://www.bbc.co.uk/news/uk-scotland-glasgow-west-47330774* (Accessed 23 February 2019).

BBC News (2019) *Tina Malone Admits 'Bulger Killer Photo' Facebook Post* [Online]. Available at *https://www.bbc.co.uk/news/uk-england-merseyside-47553107* (Accessed 13 March 2019).

Big Issue North (2015) *They Don't Scare Me Now* [Online]. Available at *https://www.bigissuenorth.com/magazine/2015/08/they-dont-scare-me-now/* (Accessed 20 April 2016).

Blair, A. (2011) *A Journey*, London, The Random House Group, Cornerstone Publishing.

Bonadio, E. (2019) *Banksy Finally Goes to Court to Stop Unauthorised Merchandising, Despite Saying Copyright Is for Losers* [Online]. Available at *https://theconversation.com/banksy-finally-goes-to-court-to-stop-unauthorised-merchandising-despite-saying-copyright-is-for-losers-112390* (Accessed 12 May 2019).

Brett Wilson (2019) *Brexiteer Ordered to Pay Philosopher £20,000 in Libel Damage for Paedophile Tweet* [Online]. Available at *https://www.brettwilson.co.uk/blog/brexiteer-ordered-to-pay-philosopher-20000-in-libel-damages-for-paedophile-tweet/* (Accessed 29 March 2019).

Carrel, S. (2016) *Labour MP Cleared of Kicking Scottish Independence Campaigner* [Online]. Available at *https://www.theguardian.com/uk-news/2016/nov/02/labour-mp-cleared-of-kicking-scottish-independence-campaigner-marie-rimmer* (Accessed 9 August 2019).

Carruthers Law (2013) *Lord McAlpine of West Green v Sally Bercow* [Online]. Available at *http://www.carruthers-law.co.uk/news/lord-mcalpine-of-west-green-v-sally-bercow/#.Vdcl3flVhBd* (Accessed 17 March 2016).

Carter, C. (2013) *Steps star H Wins Public Apology after Being Wrongly Pictured as Paedophile* [Online]. Available at *http://www.telegraph.co.uk/news/uknews/law-and-order/10527588/Steps-star-H-wins-public-apology-after-being-wrongly-pictured-as-paedophile.html* (Accessed 1 April 2016).

Civil Aviation Authority (2015) *Unmanned Aircraft and Drones* [Online]. Available at *http://www.caa.co.uk/Consumers/Unmanned-aircraft-and-drones/* (Accessed 2 March 2019).

Court of Justice of the European Union (2019) *Advocate General's Opinion in Case C-507/17, Google v CNIL.* pdf [Online]. Available at *https://curia.europa.eu/jcms/upload/docs/application/pdf/2019-01/cp190002en.pdf* (Accessed 1 July 2019).

Courts and Tribunals Judiciary (2016) *Economou v de Freitas [2016] EWHC 1853 (QB)).* [Online]. Available at *https://www.bailii.org/ew/cases/EWCA/Civ/2018/2591.html* (Accessed 4 March 2019).

Courts and Tribunals Judiciary (2017) EWHC 2992 (QB) pdf [Online]. Available at . *https://www.judiciary.uk/wp-content/uploads/2019/05/2019-EWCA-Civ-852-Serafin-v-Malkiewicz-and-ors.pdf* (Accessed 9 August 2019).

Courts and Tribunals Judiciary (2018) *Sir Cliff Richard OBE v BBC* [Online]. Available at *https://www.judiciary.uk/judgments/sir-cliff-richard-obe-v-bbc/* (Accessed 7 August 2019).

Courts and Tribunals Judiciary (2019) *Arcadia Group Limited, Topshop/Topman Limited and Sir Philip Green v Telegraph Media Group Limited (Discontinuance)* [Online]. Available at *https://www.judiciary.uk/judgments/arcadia-group-limited-topshop-topman-limited-and-sir-philip-green-v-telegraph-media-group-limited-discontinuance/* (Accessed 7 August 2019).

Courts and Tribunals Judiciary (2019) *Committals for Contempt of Court at the Royal Courts of Justice: McKeag, Barker* [Online]. Available at *https://www.judiciary.uk/wp-content/uploads/2019/02/mckeag-barker-committal-announcement-31-jan-2019.pdf* (Accessed 2 February 2019).

Courts and Tribunals Judiciary (2019) *Liberty Judgment Final* pdf [Online]. Available at *https://www.judiciary.uk/wp-content/uploads/2019/07/Liberty-judgment-Final.pdf* (Accessed 9 August 2019).

Courts and Tribunals Judiciary (2019) *President's Guidance: Guidance as to Reporting in the Family Courts* pdf [Online]. Available at *https://www.judiciary.uk/wp-content/uploads/2019/05/Presidents-Guidance-reporting-restrictions.pdf* (Accessed 9 August 2019).

Courts and Tribunals Judiciary (2019) *Richard Burgon MP v News Corp and Thomas Newton Dunn* [Online.] Available at: *https://www.judiciary.uk/judgments/richard-burgon-mp-v-news-group-newspapers-limited-thomas-zoltan-newton-dunn/* (Accessed 25 July 2019).

CPS (2009) *Contempt of Court and Reporting Restrictions: Strict Liability Contempt under the Contempt of Court Act 1981* [Online]. Available at *http://www.cps.gov.uk/legal/a_to_c/contempt_of_court/#a12* (Accessed 21 August 2015).

Dearden, L. (2018) *Man Who Taught Girlfriend's Pet Pug to Perform Nazi Salutes Fined £800* [Online]. Available at *https://www.independent.co.uk/news/uk/crime/count-dankula-nazi-pug-salutes-mark-meechan-fine-sentenced-a8317751.html* (Accessed 20 March 2019).

Defamation Update (n.d.) *The Solicitors Journal/Cases of the Week/Hird v Wood* .pdf [Online]. Available at *http://defamationupdate.co.nz/sites/all/pdf/CaseoftheMonth/Hird-v-Wood-1894-38-SJ-234.pdf* (Accessed 13 April 2016).

ECtHR (2015) *Delfi AS v Estonia* [Online]. Available at *http://hudoc.echr.coe.int/eng?i=001-155105* (Accessed 9 August 2019).

EUR-Lex (2012) *Infopaq International A/S v Danske Dagblades Forening* [Online]. pdf available at *https://eur-lex.europa.eu/legal-content/EN/TXT/?uri=CELEX:62010CO0302* (Accessed 31 July 2019).

EUR-Lex (2014) *BestWater International GmbH v Michael Mebes, Stefan Potsch* [Online]. Available at *https://eur-lex.europa.eu/legal-content/EN/TXT/?uri=CELEX%3A62013CB0348* (Accessed 18 April 2019).

European Court of Human Rights (2013*) Case of Putistin v Ukraine* [Online]. Available at *http://hudoc.echr.coe.int/eng?i=001-128204#{"itemid":["001-128204"]}* (Accessed 24 August 2015).

European Union (2018) *General Data Protection Regulation* [Online]. Available at *https://eugdpr.org/* (Accessed 23 June 2019).

Facebook (2016) *Campaigner Tells Court She Did Not Provoke Alleged Kick* [Online]. Available at *https://www.facebook.com/sthelensstar/posts/1180474945332525* (Accessed 5 January 2017).

Facebook (2018) *Government Requests For User Data* [Online]. Available at *https://transparency.facebook.com/government-data-requests* (Accessed8 August 2019).

Freedom House (2017), *New Report: Freedom of the Press 2017 – Press Freedom's Dark Horizon* [Online]. Available at *https://freedomhouse.org/article/new-report-freedom-press-2017-press-freedom-s-dark-horizon* (Accessed 22 April 2019).

Goodwin, B., (2018) *Liberty Heads for Judicial Review over Investigatory Powers Act* [Online]. Available at *https://www.computerweekly.com/news/252453696/Liberty-heads-for-judicial-review-over-Investigatory-Powers-Act* (Accessed 22 June 2019).

GOV.UK (2002) *EU Electronic Commerce Directive (ECD) Regulations* [Online]. Available at *https://www.gov.uk/government/publications/onshoring-of-elements-of-the-e-commerce-directive-relating-to-financial-services/e-commerce-directive-statement-explanatory-information* (Accessed 2 March 2019).

GOV.UK (2013) *Defamation Act 2013* [Online]. Available at *http://www.legislation.gov.uk/ukpga/2013/26* (Accessed 5 January 2017).

GOV.UK (2014) *Changes to Copyright Law*. pdf [Online] Available at *https://www.gov.uk/government/publications/changes-to-copyright-law* (Accessed 5 January 2017).

GOV.UK (2017) *The Policing and Crime Act 2017 (Consequential Amendments) Regulations 2018 (2018 No. 226)*. [Online]. Available at *https://www.legislation.gov.uk/uksi/2018/226/contents/made* (Accessed 15 July 2019).

GOV.UK (2018) *Data Protection Act 2018*. [Online]. Available at *http://www.legislation.gov.uk/ukpga/2018/12/part/6/crossheading/the-special-purposes/enacted* (Accessed 17 July 2019).

GOV.UK (2018) *European Union (Withdrawal) Act 2019* [Online]. Available at *http://www.legislation.gov.uk/ukpga/2019/16/contents/enacted* (Accessed 2 March 2019).

GOV.UK (2019) *Changes to Design and Trademark Law if the UK Leaves the EU without a Deal* [Online]. Available at *https://www.gov.uk/government/publications/changes-to-design-and-trade-mark-law-if-the-uk-leaves the-eu-without-a-deal* (Accessed 25 March 2019).

GOV.UK (2019) *Data Protection Act 2018* [Online]. Available at *https://www.gov.uk/government/collections/data-protection-act-2018* (Accessed 12 May 2019).

GOV.UK (2019) *New Media Guidance Issued to All Court Staff* [Online]. Available at https://www.gov.uk/government/news/new-media-guidance-issued-to-all-court-staff (Accessed 27 February 2019).

GOV.UK (2019) *The Intellectual Property (Copyright and Related Rights) (Amendment) (EU Exit) Regulations* [Online]. Available at https://www.legislation.gov.uk/uksi/2019/605/contents/made (Accessed 1 July 2019).

GOV.UK (2019) *Trademarks and Designs if There's no Brexit Deal* [Online] Available at https://www.gov.uk/government/publications/trade-marks-and-designs-if-theres-no-brexit-deal (Accessed 15 June 2019).

GOV.UK (2019), *IP and Brexit: The Facts* [Online]. Available at https://www.gov.uk/government/publications/ip-and-brexit-the-facts (Accessed 2 July 2019).

GOV.UK (n.d.) *Intellectual Property Office IPO* [Online]. Available at https://www.gov.uk/government/organisations/intellectual-property-office (Accessed 25 August 2015).

HoldtheFrontPage (2014) *Internet Troll Jailed for Abusing Journalist* [Online]. Available at https://www.holdthefrontpage.co.uk/2014/news/internet-troll-jailed-for-abusing-journalist/ (Accessed 25 April 2019).

HoldtheFrontPage (2016) *Wrightson Judge Explains Why He Kept Killers' Names Secret* [Online]. Available at http://www.holdthefrontpage.co.uk/2016/news/wrightson-judge-explains-why-he-kept-killers-names-secret/ (Accessed 13 April 2016).

HoldtheFrontPage (2018) *Journalist Hits Back at Trolls after Immigration Column Sparked Personal Abuse* [Online]. Available at https://www.holdthefrontpage.co.uk/2018/news/daily-journalist-hits-back-at-trolls-after-abuse-over-immigration-column/ (Accessed 24 October 2018).

HoldtheFrontPage (2019) *Journalist Claims Court Staff Trying to Intimidate Her Because She Is 'Young and Female'* [Online]. Available at *https://www.holdthefrontpage.co.uk/2019/news/journalist-claims-court-staff-trying-to-intimidate-her-because-she-is-young-and-female/* (Accessed 27 February 2019).

Holdthefrontpage (2019) *Weekly Entitled to Rely on Inaccurate Police Press Release, Rules Ipso* [Online]. Available at *https://www.holdthefrontpage.co.uk/2019/news/weekly-was-entitled-to-rely-on-inaccurate-police-press-release-ipso-rules/* (Accessed 7 May 2019).

HoldtheFrontPage.co.uk (2018) *Judge Abandons Crown Court Trial Due to Comment on Regional Press Story* [Online]. Available at *https://www.holdthefrontpage.co.uk/2018/news/judge-abandons-crown-court-trial-due-to-comment-on-regional-press-story/* (Accessed 4 September 2018).

IALS (2017) *Journalists' Sources, Surveillance and Whistleblowing* [Online]. Available at *http://dev-ials.sas.ac.uk/research/research-centres/information-law-policy-centre/research/journalists%E2%80%99-sources-surveillance* (Accessed 31 July 2019).

IALS (2017) *Protecting Sources and Whistleblowers in a Digital Age pdf.* [Online]. Available at *https://infolawcentre.blogs.sas.ac.uk/files/2017/02/Sources-Report_webversion_22_2_17.pdf* (Accessed 28 June 2019).

ICO (2016) *Data Protection and Journalism: A Guide for the Media* pdf [Online]. Available at *https://ico.org.uk/media/for-organisations/documents/1552/data-protection-and-journalism-media-guidance.pdf* (Accessed 3 March 2019).

ICO (2018) *Data Protection and Journalism: How to Complain about Media Organisations* [Online]. Available at *https://ico.org.uk/your-data-matters/data-protection-and-journalism/* (Accessed 25 May 2019).

ICO (2018) *Guide to the General Data Protection Regulation (GDPR)* [Online]. Available at *https://ico.org.uk/for-organisations/guide-to-data-protection/guide-to-the-general-data-protection-regulation-gdpr/exemptions/* (Accessed 22 June 2019).

ICO (2018) *In the Picture: A Data Protection Code of Practice for Surveillance Cameras and Personal Information.* pdf. [Online]. Available at *https://ico.org.uk/media/for-organisations/documents/1542/cctv-code-of-practice.pdf* (Accessed 14 June 2019).

ICO (2018) *Social Media Privacy Settings* [Online]. Available at *https://ico.org.uk/your-data-matters/online/social-media-privacy-settings/* (Accessed 25 March 2019).

ICO (2018) *When Can We Refuse a Request for Information?* [Online]. Available at *https://ico.org.uk/for-organisations/guide-to-freedom-of-information/refusing-a-request/* (Accessed 12 July 2019).

ICO (2019) *Blog: Cookies – what does 'good' look like?* [Online]. Available at *https://ico.org.uk/about-the-ico/news-and-events/news-and-blogs/2019/07/blog-cookies-what-does-good-look-like/* (Accessed 13 August 2019).

ICO (2019) *Bounty UK Fined £400,000 for Sharing Personal Data Unlawfully* [Online]. Available at *https://ico.org.uk/about-the-ico/news-and-events/news-and-blogs/2019/04/bounty-uk-fined-400-000-for-sharing-personal-data-unlawfully/* (Accessed 5 May 2019).

ICO (2019) *Guide to Data Protection* [Online]. Available at *https://ico.org.uk/for-organisations/guide-to-data-protection/* (Accessed 2 June 2019).

ICO (n.d.) *Exemptions* [Online]. Available at *https://ico.org.uk/for-organisations/guide-to-data-protection/guide-to-the-general-data-protection-regulation-gdpr/exemptions/* (Accessed 12 August 2019).

InfoCuria – Case-law of the Court of Justice (2015) *Pez Hejduk v EnergieAgentur. NRW GmbH, Case C-441/13* [Online]. Available at *http://curia.europa.eu/juris/document/document.jsf?docid=161611&doclang=EN* (Accessed 25 August 2015).

InfoCuria – Case-law of the Court of Justice (2016) *Case C-160/15 GS Media BV v Sanoma Media Netherlands BV, Playboy Enterprises International Inc., Britt Geertruida Dekker* [Online]. Available at *http://curia.europa.eu/juris/document/document.jsf?text=&docid=175626 &pageIndex=0&doclang=EN&mode=req&dir=&occ=first&part=1&cid =909494* (Accessed 20 April 2016).

Information Tribunal (2015) *Appeal No: EA/2014/0265)* pdf [Online]. Available at *http://www.informationtribunal.gov.uk/DBFiles/Decision/i1527/Wall,%2 0Tom%20EA.2014.0265%20%2813.04.15%29.pdf* (Accessed 20 April 2016).

Information Tribunal (2016) *Steve Pritchard and Information Commissioner EA/2015/0175.* pdf [Online]. Available at *http://www.informationtribunal.gov.uk/DBFiles/Decision/i1750/Pritchard, Steve%20EA-2015-0175%20(11-03-16-%20OPEN)%20.pdf* (Accessed 5 April 2016).

Inforrm (2015) *News: Prominent British Hindu Wins £45,000 Damages over Hindu Priest's Defamatory Emails* [Online]. Available at *https://inforrm.org/2015/01/10/news-prominent-british-hindu-wins-45000-damages-over-hindu-priests-defamatory-emails-hardeep-singh/* (Accessed 2 August 2019).

Inforrm (2015) *Sharma v Sharma Approved Judgment* pdf [Online]. Available at *https://inforrm.org/wp-content/uploads/2015/01/sharma-v-sharma-approved-jgmt-15-07-14.doc* (Accessed 9 August 2019).

Inforrm (2018) *NT1 and NT2 v Google Inc: How to Seek the Delisting of Search Engine Results Following the First English Decision on the 'Right to be Forgotten'* [Online]. Available at *https://inforrm.org/2018/04/20/nt1-and-nt2-v-google-inc-how-to-seek-the-delisting-of-search-engine-results-following-the-first-english-decision-on-the-right-to-be-forgotten/* (Accessed 25 April 2019).

Inforrm (2019) *Case Law: Serafin v Malkiewicz, Public Interest Defence Considered Again, and Judicial Unfairness* [Online]. Available at https://inforrm.org/2019/06/14/case-law-serafin-v-malkiewicz-public-interest-defence-considered-again-judicial-unfairness-samuel-rowe/ (Accessed 14 June 2019).

Inforrm (2019) *Case Law: Suttle v Walker, Facebook "Keyboard Warrior" Ordered to Pay £55,000 Libel and Harassment Damages* [Online]. Available at https://inforrm.org/2019/01/30/case-law-suttle-v-walker-facebook-keyboard-warrior-order-to-pay-55000-libel-and-harassment-damages-iain-wilson/ (Accessed 4 March 2019).

Inforrm (2019) *Case Law: ZXC v Bloomberg, Publication of Investigation into Businessman Was a Misuse of Private Information* [Online]. Available at https://inforrm.org/2019/06/03/case-law-zxc-v-bloomberg-publication-of-investigation-into-businessman-was-a-misuse-of-private-information-nathan-capone/ (Accessed 7 August 2019).

Inforrm (2019) *Morgan v Associated Newspapers: Libel Claim Settled with Apology, Substantial Charity Payment and Statement in Open Court, Four Lessons Learned for Libel Practitioners Index* [Online]. Available at https://inforrm.org/2019/02/20/morgan-v-associated-newspapers-libel-claim-settled-with-apology-substantial-charity-payment-and-statement-in-open-court-4-lessons-learned-for-libel-practitioners-matt-himsworth/ (Accessed 1 March 2019).

Inforrm (2019) *News: Supreme Court grants permission to appeal in the Morrisons mass data breach case* [Online]. Available at https://inforrm.org/2019/05/03/news-supreme-court-grants-permission-to-appeal-in-the-morrisons-mass-data-breach-case/ (Accessed 3 May 2019).

Ipso (2015) *07063-15 House v Express.co.uk* [Online]. Available at https://www.ipso.co.uk/rulings-and-resolution-statements/ruling/?id=07063-15 (Accessed 9 August 2019).

Ipso (2016) *The External Ipso Review, Sir Joseph Pilling* [Online]. Available at https://www.ipso.co.uk/media/1278/ipso_review_online.pdf (Accessed 22 April 2019).

Ipso (2017) *19498-17 Perrin v The News (Portsmouth)* [Online]. Available at *https://www.ipso.co.uk/rulings-and-resolution-statements/ruling/?id=19498-17* (Accessed 25 April 2019).

Ipso (2019) *05768-18 Solomon v Mail Online* [Online]. Available at *https://www.ipso.co.uk/rulings-and-resolution-statements/ruling/?id=05768-18* (Accessed 1 April 2019).

Ipso (2019) *07908-18 A Woman v theargus.co.uk* [Online]. Available at *https://www.ipso.co.uk/rulings-and-resolution-statements/ruling/?id=07908-18* (Accessed 22 March 2019).

Ipso (2019) *Editors' Code of Practice* [Online]. Available at: *https://www.ipso.co.uk/editors-code-of-practice/* (Accessed 2 April 2019).

Lexology (2019) *Do Professionals Have the 'Right to be Forgotten'?* [Online]. Available at *https://www.lexology.com/library/detail.aspx?g=07c17b01-7c3d-47cd-8200-5db540c2b6eb* (Accessed 22 April 2019).

Lexology (2019) *Google Ordered to Pay First Multi-Million GDPR Fine* [Online]. Available at *https://www.lexology.com/library/detail.aspx?g=1b96ecc5-2657-48b6-830b-73f810d8353a&utm_source=Lexology+Daily+Newsfeed&utm_medium=HTML+email+-+Body+-+General+section&utm_campaign=Lexology+subscriber+daily+feed&utm_content=Lexology+Daily+Newsfeed+2019-03-11&utm_term=* (Accessed 19 May 2019).

Lexology (2019) *How Much Information is Enough Information? CJEU Asked to Rule on the Extent of Online Platforms' Responsibility to Copyright Holders* [Online]. Available at *https://www.lexology.com/library/detail.aspx?g=25ba0ded-1cc2-4b72-bd04-141c4262d409* (Accessed 23 June 2019).

Lexology (2019) *Panini Cheapskates: Straight Infringement for a 'Wonky' Parody* [Online]. Available at *https://www.lexology.com/library/detail.aspx?g=723d841d-89aa-41a7-a430-7ac6e2bc98d4* (Accessed 28 February 2019).

Matrix Chambers, 2017, *Claim Against Facebook for the Misuse of Private Information* [Online]. Available at *https://www.matrixlaw.co.uk/judgments/claim-facebook-misuse-private-information/* (Accessed 9 August 2019).

Matrix Chambers (2017) *Matrix Launches 'Online Publication Claims: A Practical Guide'* [Online]. Available at *https://www.matrixlaw.co.uk/news/matrix-launches-online-publication-claims-practical-guide/* (Accessed 9 August 2019).

Mayhew, F. (2017) *Freelance Photographer Sues Sky News after it Refuses to Pay for Image Used in Embedded Twitter Message* [Online]. Available at *https://www.pressgazette.co.uk/freelance-photographer-sues-sky-news-after-it-refuses-to-pay-for-image-used-in-embedded-twitter-message/* (Accessed 2 March 2019).

Mayhew, F. (2019) *European Publishers Welcome New Digital Copyright Directive Passed by EU Parliament* [Online]. Available at *https://www.pressgazette.co.uk/eu-parliament-passes-new-digital-copyright-directive/* (Accessed 25 July 2019).

Mayhew, F. (2019) *New EU Copyright Deal Will Allow Facebook and Google to Share 'Very Short' News Snippets Only* [Online]. Available at *https://www.pressgazette.co.uk/new-eu-copyright-deal-will-allow-facebook-and-google-to-share-very-short-news-snippets/* (Accessed 15 May 2019).

Mayhew, F. (2019) *Online Harms White Paper* [Online]. Available at *https://www.pressgazette.co.uk/press-freedom-concerns-raised-over-online-harms-white-paper-as-details-leak/* (Accessed 26 March 2019).

National Constitution Center (n.d.) *Amendment I Freedom of Religion, Speech, Press, Assembly, and Petition* [Online]. Available at *https://constitutioncenter.org/interactive-constitution/amendments/amendment-i* (Accessed 21 August 2015).

Net Litigation (1996) *Shetland Times, Ltd. v Jonathan Wills and Another* [Online]. Available at *http://www.netlitigation.com/netlitigation/cases/shetland.htm* (Accessed 20 April 2016).

O'Carroll, L. (2014) *Plebgate: Met Obtained Phone Records of Sun Political Editor without Consent* [Online]. Available at *http://www.theguardian.com/media/2014/sep/02/plebgate-met-phone-records-sun-tom-newton-dunn* (Accessed 24 August 2015).

O'Carroll, L. (2014) *Police Secretly Obtained Reporter's Phone Records in Huhne Investigation* [Online]. Available at *http://www.theguardian.com/uk-news/2014/oct/05/police-chris-huhne-reporter-phone-records* (Accessed 24 August 2015).

Ofcom (2018) *Ofcom's annual report on the BBC* pdf [Online]. Available at *https://www.ofcom.org.uk/__data/assets/pdf_file/0015/124422/BBC-annual-report.pdf* (Accessed 13 August 2019).

Office for National Statistics (2019) *Crime in England and Wales: year ending March 2019* [Online]. Available at *https://www.ons.gov.uk/peoplepopulationandcommunity/crimeandjustice/bulletins/crimeinenglandandwales/yearendingmarch2019#decrease-in-computer-viruses-continues-to-drive-the-fall-in-computer-misuse-offences* (Accessed 16 August 2019).

PA Media Lawyer (2019) *Contempt risk remains for released suspects still 'under investigation' by police after law change* [Online]. Available at *https://www.pressgazette.co.uk/contempt-risk-for-suspects-released-as-under-investigation-by-police-after-law-change/* (Accessed 12 August 2019).

Perraudin, F. (2016) *Former Sun Editor Convicted over Adam Johnson Victim Picture* [Online]. Available at *https://www.theguardian.com/uk-news/2016/mar/07/adam-johnson-former-sun-editor-david-dinsmore-convicted-victim-picture* (Accessed 25 July 2019).

Pinsent Masons (2018) Defamation claims on the rise in London [Online]. Available at *https://www.pinsentmasons.com/out-law/news/defamation-claims-rise-london* (Accessed 13 August 2019).

Pinsent Masons (2019) *UK Approach on EU Copyright Reforms Depends on Brexit* [Online]. Available at *https://www.pinsentmasons.com/out-law/news/uk-eu-copyright-reforms-brexit* (Accessed 21 June 2019).

Ponsford, D. (2017) *'David and Goliath' Legal Battle Sees Rochdale Online Win Legal Battle from Manchester Evening News over Danczuk Expenses Story* [Online]. Available at http://www.pressgazette.co.uk/david-and-goliath-legal-battle-sees-rochdale-online-win-payout-from-manchester-evening-news-over-lifted-news-story/ (Accessed 29 April 2019).

Ponsford, D. (2017) *Independent Declines to Pay for Court Story 'Lifted' from Wales Online Telling Freelance: 'There Is No Copyright in News'* [Online]. Available at http://www.pressgazette.co.uk/independent-declines-to-pay-for-court-story-lifted-from-wales-online-telling-freelance-there-is-no-copyright-in-news/ (Accessed 29 April 2019).

Reporters without Borders (2019) *2019 World Press Freedom Index* [Online]. Available at https://rsf.org/en/ranking (Accessed 4 May 2019).

Shoffman, M., (2006) *Ashley Cole Files Lawsuit over Gay Orgy Story* [Online]. (Available at http://www.pinknews.co.uk/2006/03/03/ashley-cole-files-lawsuit-over-gay-orgy-story/ (Accessed 21 August 2015).

Smith, M., (2018) *Updating Our 'Right to be Forgotten' Transparency Report* [Online]. Available at https://www.blog.google/around-the-globe/google-europe/updating-our-right-be-forgotten-transparency-report/ (Accessed 18 June 2019).

Taylor Wessing (2019) *CJEU Rules That Knowingly Linking to Illegal Content Infringes Copyright* [Online]. Available at https://united-kingdom.taylorwessing.com/en/cjeu-rules-that-knowingly-linking-to-illegal-content-infringes-copyright (Accessed 23 May 2019).

The Guardian (1999) *Aitken Jailed for 18 Months* [Online]. Available at http://www.theguardian.com/politics/1999/jun/08/uk (Accessed 8 April 2016).

Thom, C. (2015) *Tom Wall Has Won a Freedom of Information Battle in a War That Journalists Should Not Have to Fight* [Online]. Available at https://www.pressgazette.co.uk/tom-wall-has-won-a-freedom-of-information-battle-in-a-war-that-journalists-should-not-have-to-fight/ (Accessed 9 August 2019).

Thom, C. (2016) *When Government Press Officers Think They Are Court Reporters Justice Could Be the Loser* [Online]. Available at http://www.pressgazette.co.uk/journalists-beware-of-government-press-officers-who-think-they-are-court-reporters/ (Accessed 5 January 2017).

Tobitt, C. (2019) *Tory MP Wins Libel Payout from Sunday Times over 'Utterly Unfounded' Sex Misconduct Claims* [Online]. Available at https://www.pressgazette.co.uk/tory-mp-wins-libel-payout-from-sunday-times-over-utterly-unfounded-sex-misconduct-claims/ (Accessed 5 May 2019).

Tomlinson, H. and Vassall-Adams, G. (eds) (2017) *Online Publications Claims: A Guide*, London: Matrix Chambers.

Twitter (2018) *Transparency Report: Information Requests* [Online]. Available at https://transparency.twitter.com/en/information-requests.html (Accessed 25 April 2019).

UK Legislation (n.d.) *Copyright, Designs and Patents Act 1988* [Online]. Available at http://www.legislation.gov.uk/ukpga/1988/48/contents (Accessed 25 August 2015).

UK Legislation (n.d.) *Criminal Justice and Courts Act 2015* [Online]. Available at http://www.legislation.gov.uk/ukpga/2015/2/section/72/enacted (Accessed 21 August 2015).

UK Legislation (n.d.) *Defamation Act 2013* [Online]. Available at http://www.legislation.gov.uk/ukpga/2013/26/contents (Accessed 24 August 2015).

UK Legislation (n.d.) *Human Rights Act 1998 Article 10* [Online]. Available at http://www.legislation.gov.uk/ukpga/1998/42/schedule/1/part/1/chapter/2 (Accessed 21 August 2015).

UK Legislation (n.d.) *Terrorism Act 2000* [Online]. Available at http://www.legislation.gov.uk/ukpga/2000/11/section/44 (Accessed 25 August 2015).

UK Parliament House of Lords (n.d.) *Judgments – Reynolds v Times Newspapers Limited and Others* [Online]. Available at *http://www.publications.parliament.uk/pa/ld199899/ldjudgmt/jd991028/rey01.htm* (Accessed 21 August 2015).

Vaizey, E. (2016) *Social Networking: Photographs* [Online]. Available at *http://www.theyworkforyou.com/wrans/?id=2015-10-19.12484.h&s=speaker%3A11905#g12484.r0* (Accessed 30 March 2016).

Walker, P. (2019) *YouTuber Accused of Triggering Rape Threats Could Stand for UKIP* [Online]. Available at *https://www.theguardian.com/politics/2019/mar/22/youtuber-carl-benjamin-accused-triggering-rape-threats-could-stand-for-ukip* (Accessed 25 March 2019).

WhatDoTheyKnow (n.d.) *Browse and Search Requests* [Online]. Available at *https://www.whatdotheyknow.com/list/all?#results* (Accessed 25 August 2015).

Wired Gov (2015) *ICO Orders Removal of Google Search Results* [Online]. Available at *https://www.wired-gov.net/wg/news.nsf/articles/ICO+orders+removal+of+Google+search+results+21082015152500?open* (Accessed 31 July 2019).

47380711R00114

Printed in Poland
by Amazon Fulfillment
Poland Sp. z o.o., Wrocław